CORNERSTONES

CORNERSTONES

OF SLOVENIA'S NATO MEMBERSHIP

EURO-ATLANTIC SECURITY STUDIES SERIES

Edited by Boštjan Šinkovec

iUniverse, Inc.

New York Lincoln Shanghai

CORNERSTONES
OF SLOVENIA'S NATO MEMBERSHIP

iUniverse, Inc.

For information address:
iUniverse
2021 Pine Lake Road, Suite 100
Lincoln, NE 68512
www.iuniverse.com

The front cover photograph by Matthew Fynch

ISBN: 0-595-27969-4

Printed in the United States of America

This book is dedicated to my dad, a Science Fiction fan, who has believed as long as I can remember that NATO membership is vital for Slovenian sovereignty.

I would also like to thank those who have helped me gather the public documents on NATO, especially Andrej Slapničar, and Mateja Kunovar for the scanning of documents.

CONTENTS:

FOREWORD

During the days of the NATO, or should I say, anti-NATO membership campaign in Slovenia that burst out in the Summer of 2001 and has not really ended, in spite of the referendum victory of 23 March 2003, it became very obvious, following the arguments and counter-arguments used in the mud-slinging, that the debate had not much to do with what NATO was actually all about.

The problem I saw was not that the very loud minority opposing Slovenia's membership in the North Atlantic Alliance used slander, blatant lies as well as disqualifications, but that the other side very often had no idea why it was important for Slovenia to become a member, what NATO was based on, how it operated and how it was still relevant in the post Cold War and post 9/11 world.

I first learned about NATO from my dad who was probably the first Slovenian who proposed that Slovenia should join NATO, at the time when Slovenia was still part of another country, and a totalitarian one at that. Later on he got professionally involved in Slovenia's drive towards NATO membership. Being in touch with the matter on a daily basis, in spite of dad trying to spare us from his burden, I sort of naturally decided to study international affairs and focus on security issues.

Signing of the accession protocol for Slovenia is not something that happened overnight. While the first contacts with NATO were made around the time of Slovenia's independence, the first formal step was membership in the Partnership for Peace in 1994 followed by participation in the Planning and Review Process. In 1995 Slovenia signed the PfP SOFA agreement and concluded the IFOR transit agreement with NATO. After it had become a member of the North Atlantic Cooperation Council it became the first partner country to start its Individual Dialogue with NATO, with a view to present itself as a credible candidate for Alliance membership.

After three rounds of the Individual Dialogue Slovenia entered the Membership Action Plan, completed three rounds of its Annual National Programmes and started on the fourth one. The November 2002 Prague Summit rewarded the efforts by issuing an invitation to Slovenia to start accession talks with NATO. After the successful completion of two rounds of talks in early 2003 the stage was set for the signing of the Accession Protocol, and hopefully we will be able to say that the rest is history.

Following the NATO membership debate before the NATO referendum in Slovenia I realized that what both sides needed was actually basic information on NATO and what Slovenia's membership would mean both to Slovenia and to the Alliance.

That was the reason for the compilation of the documents that are actually in the public domain, but in spite of their availability somehow escape the eye of the people that need them most.

This compilation includes every international agreement Slovenia will have to adhere to, but one, either to be able to join, such as the Washington Treaty, or to be able to fulfil its rights and obligations. The latter will be acceded to in the post-membership period.

The second batch of documents represents those that have made enlargement with Slovenia and other states possible, such as the Study on Enlargement or the Washington Summit Declaration.

I thought of including a number of Slovenian political statements, speeches as well as documents released to the public, including the so-called Timetable of the Republic of Slovenia for the Completion of Reforms, which represents an attachment to the letter of the Minister of Foreign Affairs of Slovenia sent to the NATO Secretary General before the 19 members of the North Atlantic Council signed the Accession Protocol for Slovenia, to demonstrate the steps countries have to make to enter NATO. However, because of the growing bulk of documents I decided to separate the latter from the general "NATO" documents and attempt to publish them separately under the title "Milestones" in the near future. While "Cornerstones" is very much a general look at the enlargement "Milestones" will be specifically focused on Slovenia.

I expect, or rather hope that the book will find its purpose.

Boštjan Šinkovec, Brussels, 30 April 2003

The North Atlantic Treaty

Washington D.C.—4 April 1949

The Parties to this Treaty reaffirm their faith in the purposes and principles of the Charter of the United Nations and their desire to live in peace with all peoples and all governments.
They are determined to safeguard the freedom, common heritage and civilisation of their peoples, founded on the principles of democracy, individual liberty and the rule of law. They seek to promote stability and well-being in the North Atlantic area.
They are resolved to unite their efforts for collective defence and for the preservation of peace and security. They therefore agree to this North Atlantic Treaty:

Article 1

The Parties undertake, as set forth in the Charter of the United Nations, to settle any international dispute in which they may be involved by peaceful means in such a manner that international peace and security and justice are not endangered, and to refrain in their international relations from the threat or use of force in any manner inconsistent with the purposes of the United Nations.

Article 2

The Parties will contribute toward the further development of peaceful and friendly international relations by strengthening their free institutions, by bringing about a better understanding of the principles upon which these institutions are founded, and by promoting conditions of stability and well-being. They will seek to eliminate conflict in their international economic policies and will encourage economic collaboration between any or all of them.

Article 3

In order more effectively to achieve the objectives of this Treaty, the Parties, separately and jointly, by means of continuous and effective self-help and mutual aid, will maintain and develop their individual and collective capacity to resist armed attack.

Article 4

The Parties will consult together whenever, in the opinion of any of them, the territorial integrity, political independence or security of any of the Parties is threatened.

Article 5

The Parties agree that an armed attack against one or more of them in Europe or North America shall be considered an attack against them all and consequently they agree that, if such an armed attack occurs, each of them, in exercise of the right of individual or collective self-defence recognised by Article 51 of the Charter of the United Nations, will assist the Party or Parties so attacked by taking forthwith, individually and in concert with the other Parties, such action as it deems necessary, including the use of armed force, to restore and maintain the security of the North Atlantic area.

Any such armed attack and all measures taken as a result thereof shall immediately be reported to the Security Council. Such measures shall be terminated when the Security Council has taken the measures necessary to restore and maintain international peace and security .

Article 6 ([1])

For the purpose of Article 5, an armed attack on one or more of the Parties is deemed to include an armed attack:
- on the territory of any of the Parties in Europe or North America, on the Algerian Departments of France ([2]), on the territory of or on the Islands under the jurisdiction of any of the Parties in the North Atlantic area north of the Tropic of Cancer;
- on the forces, vessels, or aircraft of any of the Parties, when in or over these territories or any other area in Europe in which occupation forces of any of the Parties were stationed on the date when the Treaty entered into force or the Mediterranean Sea or the North Atlantic area north of the Tropic of Cancer.

Article 7

This Treaty does not affect, and shall not be interpreted as affecting in any way the rights and obligations under the Charter of the Parties which are members of the United Nations, or the primary responsibility of the Security Council for the maintenance of international peace and security.

Article 8

Each Party declares that none of the international engagements now in force between it and any other of the Parties or any third State is in conflict with the provisions of this Treaty, and undertakes not to enter into any international engagement in conflict with this Treaty.

Article 9

The Parties hereby establish a Council, on which each of them shall be represented, to consider matters concerning the implementation of this Treaty. The Council shall be so organised as to be able to meet promptly at any time. The Council shall set up such subsidiary bodies as may be necessary; in particular it shall establish immediately a defence committee which shall recommend measures for the implementation of Articles 3 and 5.

Article 10

The Parties may, by unanimous agreement, invite any other European State in a position to further the principles of this Treaty and to contribute to the security of the North Atlantic area to accede to this Treaty. Any State so invited may become a Party to the Treaty by depositing its instrument of accession with the Government of the United States of America. The Government of the United States of America will inform each of the Parties of the deposit of each such instrument of accession.

Article 11

This Treaty shall be ratified and its provisions carried out by the Parties in accordance with their respective constitutional processes. The instruments of ratification shall be deposited as soon as possible with the Government of the United States of America, which will notify all the other signatories of each deposit. The Treaty shall enter into force between the States which have ratified it as soon as the ratifications of the majority of the signatories, including the ratifications of Belgium, Canada, France, Luxembourg, the Netherlands, the United Kingdom and the United States, have been deposited and shall come into effect with respect to other States on the date of the deposit of their ratifications. [3]

Article 12

After the Treaty has been in force for ten years, or at any time thereafter, the Parties shall, if any of them so requests, consult together for the purpose of reviewing the Treaty, having regard for the factors then affecting peace and security in the North Atlantic area, including the development of universal as well as regional arrangements under the Charter of the United Nations for the maintenance of international peace and security.

Article 13

After the Treaty has been in force for twenty years, any Party may cease to be a Party one year after its notice of denunciation has been given to the Government of the United States of America, which will inform the Governments of the other Parties of the deposit of each notice of denunciation.

Article 14
This Treaty, of which the English and French texts are equally authentic, shall be deposited in the archives of the Government of the United States of America. Duly certified copies will be transmitted by that Government to the Governments of other signatories.

Footnotes:
1. The definition of the territories to which Article 5 applies was revised by Article 2 of the Protocol to the North Atlantic Treaty on the accession of Greece and Turkey signed on 22 October 1951.
2. On January 16, 1963, the North Atlantic Council noted that insofar as the former Algerian Departments of France were concerned, the relevant clauses of this Treaty had become inapplicable as from July 3, 1962.
3. The Treaty came into force on 24 August 1949, after the deposition of the ratifications of all signatory states.

Protocol to the North Atlantic Treaty on the Accession of Greece and Turkey

The Parties to the North Atlantic Treaty, signed at Washington on April 4, 1949 Being satisfied that the security of the North Atlantic area will be enhanced by the accession of the Kingdom of Greece and the Republic of Turkey to that Treaty, agree as follows:

Article 1

Upon the entry into force of this Protocol, the Government of the United States of America shall, on behalf of all the Parties, communicate to the Government of the Kingdom of Greece and the Government of the Republic of Turkey an invitation to accede to the North Atlantic Treaty, as it may be modified by Article 2 of the present Protocol. Thereafter the Kingdom of Greece and the Republic of Turkey shall each become a Party on the date when it deposits its instruments of accession with the Government of the United States of America in accordance with Article 10 of the Treaty.

Article 2

If the Republic of Turkey becomes a Party to the North Atlantic Treaty, Article 6 of the Treaty shall, as from the date of the deposit by the Government of the Republic of Turkey of its instruments of accession with the Government of the United States of America, be modified to read as follows:

For the purpose of Article 5, an armed attack on one or more of the Parties is deemed to include an armed attack:

1. on the territory of any of the Parties in Europe or North America, on the Algerian Departments of France, on the territory of Turkey or on the islands under the jurisdiction of any of the Parties in the North Atlantic area north of the Tropic of Cancer;
2. on the forces, vessels, or aircraft of any of the Parties, when in or over these territories or any other area in Europe in which occupation forces of any of the Parties were stationed on the date when the Treaty entered into force or the Mediterranean Sea or the North Atlantic area north of the Tropic of Cancer.

Article 3

The present Protocol shall enter into force when each of the Parties to the North Atlantic Treaty has notified the Government of the United States of

America of its acceptance thereof. The Government of the United States of America shall inform all the Parties to the North Atlantic Treaty of the date of the receipt of each such notification and of the date of the entry into force of the present Protocol.

Article 4

The present Protocol, of which the English and French texts are equally authentic, shall be deposited in the Archives of the Government of the United States of America. Duly certified copies thereof shall be transmitted by that Government to the Governments of all the Parties to the North Atlantic Treaty.

October 22, 1951

Documents signed by the Parties to the North Atlantic Treaty under the terms of the Paris agreements

Paris, 22-23 October 1954

A series of conferences and ministerial meetings took place in the autumn of 1954, resulting in a set of formal agreements and undertakings by the participating countries relating to their mutual security. The documents issued at the conclusion of this period of intensive diplomatic and juridical debate are known collectively as the Paris Agreements.

The London Conference held between 28 September and 3 October 1954, also known as the Nine-Power(*) Conference, culminated in the Final Act of the Conference. However it was agreed that all the decisions of the Conference formed part of one general settlement of direct or indirect concern to all the North Atlantic Treaty Powers and would therefore be submitted to the North Atlantic Council for information or decision.

The decisions of the Conference were recorded in the following series of documents: The Final Act itself, which consisted of the following six sections:

I. A declaration by the Governments of France, the United Kingdom, and the United States on the termination of the Occupation regime in the Federal Republic of Germany;

II. Agreements between the signatories relating to the Brussels Treaty and to their intention to invite the Federal Republic of Germany and Italy to accede to the Treaty;

III. Assurances provided by the United States, the United Kingdom, and Canada relating to the extension and modification of the Brussels Treaty;

IV. Agreement among NATO participants at the Conference on recommendations to be made to the North Atlantic Council regarding the future membership of the Federal Republic of Germany and on the reinforcement of the NATO machinery; and agreement that the North Atlantic Treaty should be regarded as of indefinite duration;

V. A Declaration by the Government of the Federal Republic of Germany relating to its obligations under the Charter of the United Nations; and a Declaration by the Governments of the United States, the United Kingdom and France relating to the UN Charter and to Germany;

VI. Agreement on future procedure with regard to the implementation of the decisions of the Conference.

Annexed to the Final Act and forming part of it were a Draft Declaration and Draft Protocol to the Brussels Treaty; statements made by the Secretary of State of the United States and by the Foreign Ministers of the United Kingdom and Canada; and a Conference Paper on "A German defence contribution and arrangements to apply to SACEUR's forces on the continent". The Paris Conference took place from 20 to 22 October 1954 and was followed on 23 October by a Ministerial Meeting of the North Atlantic Council.

The Paris Agreements comprise an ensemble of documents, protocols and annexes signed by the respective Parties to the Agreements, as well as a number of declarations and exchanges of letters. The four documents signed by the Parties to the North Atlantic Treaty are reproduced below. All other formal documents which, together with the above, constitute the Paris Agreements, can be accessed on the Internet via the NATO Integrated Data Service at www.nato.int (Related International Organisations and Institutions, Western European Union (WEU), Documents, Treaties).

The Brussels Treaty, as amended by the Paris Agreements and signed on 23 October 1954, is reproduced in Part I, together with the original Treaty signed on 17 March 1948.

(*) Belgium, Canada, France, the Federal Republic of Germany, Italy, Luxembourg, the Netherlands, the United Kingdom and the United States of America.

Resolution adopted by the North Atlantic Council to implement Section IV of the Final Act of the London Conference

Paris, 22 October 1954

The North Atlantic Council:

1. Recognising the necessity of strengthening the structure of the Alliance and of reinforcing the machinery for the collective defence of Europe, and desirous of specifying the conditions governing joint examination of the defence effort of member countries.

2. Recalls that:

    a. the resources which member nations intend to devote to their defence effort as well as the level, composition and quality of the forces which the member nations are contributing to the defence of the North Atlantic area are each year subject to collective examination in the NATO Annual Review for the purpose of reaching agreement on force goals, taking into account expected mutual aid;

    b. the defence expenditures incurred by the member nations and the extent to which the recommendations emerging from the Annual Review have been carried out are the subject of periodical review during the year.

3. Agrees with the terms of the Agreement on Forces of Western European Union; and that with respect to the forces which the members of Western European Union will place under NATO Command on the mainland of Europe and for which maximum figures have been established in that Agreement, if at any time during the NATO Annual Review recommendations are put forward, the effect of which would be to increase the level of forces above the limits established in this Agreement, the acceptance by the country concerned of such recommended increases shall be subject to unanimous approval by the members of Western European Union, expressed either in the Council of Western European Union or in the North Atlantic Treaty Organisation.

4. Decides that all forces of member nations stationed in the area of the Allied Command, Europe, shall be placed under the authority of the Supreme Allied Commander, Europe, or other appropriate NATO Command and under the direction of the NATO military authorities with the exception of

those forces intended for the defence of overseas territories and other forces which the North Atlantic Treaty Organisation has recognised or will recognise as suitable to remain under national command.

5. Invites member nations to make an initial report for consideration and recognition by the Council on those forces which they plan to maintain within the area of Allied Command, Europe, for the common defence, but not to place under the authority of the North Atlantic Treaty Organisation, taking into account the provisions of relevant NATO directives bearing on that subject; the initial report will include a broad statement of the reason for which the above forces are not so placed. Thereafter, if any changes are proposed, the North Atlantic Council action on the NATO Annual Review will constitute recognition as to the suitability and size of forces to be placed under the authority of the appropriate NATO Command and those to be retained under national command.

6. Notes that the agreements concluded within the framework of the Organisation of Western European Union on the internal defence and police forces which the members of that Organisation will maintain on the mainland shall be notified to the North Atlantic Council.

7. Agrees, in the interest of most effective collective defence, that in respect of combat forces in the area of Allied Command, Europe, and under the Supreme Allied Commander, Europe:
   a. all deployments shall be in accordance with NATO strategy;
   b. the location of forces in accordance with NATO operational plans shall be determined by the Supreme Allied Commander, Europe, after consultation and agreement with the national authorities concerned;
   c. forces under the Supreme Allied Commander, Europe, and within the area of Allied Command, Europe, shall not be redeployed or used operationally within that area without the consent of the Supreme Allied Commander, Europe, subject to political guidance furnished by the North Atlantic Council, when appropriate, through normal channels.

8. Decides that:
   a. integration of forces at Army Group and Tactical Air Force level shall be maintained;
   b. in view of the powerful combat support units and logistic support organisation at Army level, integration at that level and associated Air Force level will be the rule;
   c. wherever formations of several nationalities are operating in the same area and on a common task, provided there are no overriding objections from the point of view of military effectiveness; wherever military efficiency permits, in light of the size, location and logistic support of forces,

integration at lower levels, both in the land and air forces, shall be achieved to the maximum extent possible;

d. proposals to the North Atlantic Council, indicating any increases in commonly financed items of expenditure, such as infrastructure which might be entailed by the adoption of such measures, should be submitted by the NATO military authorities.

9. Agrees that, in order to improve the capability of the Supreme Allied Commander, Europe, to discharge his responsibilities in the defence of Allied Command, Europe, his responsibilities and powers for the logistic support of the forces placed under his authority shall be extended.

10. Considers that these increased responsibilities and powers should include authority:

a. to establish, in consultation with the national authorities concerned, requirements for the provision of logistic resources;

b. to determine, in agreement with the national authorities concerned, their geographic distribution;

c. to establish, in consultation with these authorities, logistic priorities for the raising, equipping and maintenance of units;

d. to direct the utilisation, for meeting his requirements, of those portions of the logistic support systems made available to him by the appropriate authorities;

e. to coordinate and supervise the use, for logistical purposes, of NATO common infrastructure facilities and of those national facilities made available to him by the national authorities.

11. Agrees that, in order to ensure that adequate information is obtained and made available to the appropriate authorities about the forces placed under the Supreme Allied Commander, Europe, including reserve formations and their logistic support within the area of Allied Command, Europe, the Supreme Allied Commander, Europe, shall be granted increased authority to call for reports regarding the level and effectiveness of such forces and their armaments, equipment and supplies as well as the organisation and location of their logistic arrangements. He shall also make field inspections within that area as necessary.

12. Invites nations to submit to the Supreme Allied Commander, Europe, such reports to this end as he may call for from time to time; and to assist inspection within the area of Allied Command, Europe, by the Supreme Allied Commander, Europe, of these forces and their logistic support arrangements as necessary.

13. Confirms that the powers exercised by the Supreme Allied Commander, Europe, in peace-time extend not only to the organisation into an effective

integrated force of the forces placed under him but also to their training; that in this field, the Supreme Allied Commander, Europe, has direct control over the higher training of all national forces assigned to his command in peace-time; and that he should receive facilities from member nations to inspect the training of those cadre and other forces within the area of Allied Command, Europe, earmarked for that Command.

14. Directs the NATO military authorities to arrange for the designation by the Supreme Allied Commander, Europe, of a high-ranking officer of his Command who will be authorised to transmit regularly to the Council of Western European Union information relating to the forces of the members of Western European Union on the mainland of Europe acquired as a result of the reports and inspections mentioned in paragraphs 11 and 12 in order to enable that Council to establish that the limits laid down in the special agreement mentioned in paragraph 3 above are being observed.

15. Agrees that the expression "the area of Allied Command, Europe" as used throughout this Resolution shall not include North Africa; and that this Resolution does not alter the present status of the United Kingdom and United States forces in the Mediterranean.

16. Directs the NATO Military Committee to initiate the necessary changes in the directives to give effect to the above policies and objectives of the North Atlantic Council.

Resolution adopted by the North Atlantic Council on the Results of the Four-Power and Nine-Power Meetings

Paris, 22 October 1954

The North Atlantic Council:

Recognising that all the arrangements arising out of the London Conference form part of one general settlement which is directly or indirectly of concern to all the NATO Powers and has therefore been submitted to the Council for information or decision;

Have learnt with satisfaction of the arrangements agreed between the Governments of France, the United Kingdom and the United States of America and of the Federal Republic of Germany for the termination of the Occupation Regime in the Federal Republic as set forth in the Protocol communicated to the Council;

Welcome the decision of the Brussels Treaty Powers to invite the Federal Republic of Germany and Italy to accede to the Brussels Treaty as modified and completed by the Protocols and other documents communicated to the Council, and hereby record their agreement with the provisions of those Protocols and documents insofar as they concern action by the North Atlantic Treaty Organisation;

Welcome the extension of the Brussels Treaty as an important step toward the achievement of European unity; and express confidence that there will be the closest cooperation between the Western European Union and the North Atlantic Treaty Organisation which remains the foundation of the security and progress of the Atlantic Community;

Take note with satisfaction of the statements made on September 29, 1954 in London by the United States Secretary of State and the Canadian Secretary of State for External Affairs, and of the declaration by the Foreign Secretary of the United Kingdom concerning the maintenance of United Kingdom forces on the continent of Europe;

Finally,

Record their deep satisfaction at the happy conclusion of all the above arrangements which together constitute a decisive step in fortifying the North Atlantic Alliance and uniting the Free World.

Resolution of Association by Other Parties to the North Atlantic Treaty adopted by the North Atlantic Council

Paris, 22 October 1954

The North Atlantic Council:

Welcoming the declaration made in London by the Government of the Federal Republic of Germany on October 3, 1954 (Annex A), and the related declaration made on the same occasion by the Governments of the United States of America, the United Kingdom of Great Britain and Northern Ireland and the French Republic (Annex B),

Notes with satisfaction that the representatives of the other Parties to the North Atlantic Treaty have, on behalf of their Governments, today associated themselves with the aforesaid declaration of the Three Powers.

ANNEX A

DECLARATION BY THE GOVERNMENT OF THE FEDERAL REPUBLIC OF GERMANY

The Federal Republic of Germany has agreed to conduct its policy in accordance with the principles of the Charter of the United Nations and accepts the obligations set forth in Article 2 of the Charter.

Upon her accession to the North Atlantic Treaty and the Brussels Treaty, the Federal Republic of Germany declares that she will refrain from any action inconsistent with the strictly defensive character of the two Treaties. In particular, the Federal Republic of Germany undertakes never to have recourse to force to achieve the re-unification of Germany or the modification of the present boundaries of the Federal Republic of Germany, and to resolve by peaceful means any disputes which may arise between the Federal Republic and other States.

ANNEX B

DECLARATION BY THE GOVERNMENTS OF UNITED STATES OF AMERICA, UNITED KINGDOM AND FRANCE

The Governments of the United States of America, the United Kingdom of Great Britain and Northern Ireland and the French Republic,

Being resolved to devote their efforts to the strengthening of peace in accordance with the Charter of the United Nations and in particular with the obligations set forth in Article 2 of the Charter:

    i.   to settle their international disputes by peaceful means in such a manner that international peace and security and justice are not endangered;

    ii. to refrain in their international relations from the threat or use of force against the territorial integrity or political independence of any State, or in any other manner inconsistent with the purposes of the United Nations;

    iii. to give the United Nations every assistance in any action it takes in accordance with the Charter, and to refrain from giving assistance to any State against which the United Nations take preventive or enforcement action;

    iv. to ensure that States which are not Members of the United Nations act in accordance with the principles of the Charter so far as may be necessary for the maintenance of international peace and security;

Having regard to the purely defensive character of the Atlantic Alliance which is manifest in the North Atlantic Treaty, wherein they reaffirm their faith in the purposes and principles of the Charter of the United Nations and their desire to live in peace with all peoples and all Governments, and undertake to settle their international disputes by peaceful means in accordance with the principles of the Charter and to refrain, in accordance with those principles, from the threat or use of force in their international relations;

Take note that the Federal Republic of Germany has by a Declaration dated 3 October 1954 accepted the obligations set forth in Article 2 of the Charter of the United Nations and has undertaken never to have recourse to force to achieve the unification of Germany or the modification of the present boundaries of the Federal Republic of Germany, and to resolve by peaceful means any disputes which may arise between the Federal Republic and other States;

Declare that:

1. They consider the Government of the Federal Republic as the only German Government freely and legitimately constituted and therefore entitled to

speak for Germany as the representative of the German people in international affairs.

2. In their relations with the Federal Republic they will follow the principles set out in Article 2 of the United Nations Charter.

3. A peace settlement for the whole of Germany, freely negotiated between Germany and her former enemies, which should lay the foundation of a lasting peace, remains an essential aim of their policy. The final determination of the boundaries of Germany must await such a settlement.

4. The achievement through peaceful means of a fully free and unified Germany remains a fundamental goal of their policy.

5. The security and welfare of Berlin and the maintenance of the position of the Three Powers there are regarded by the Three Powers as essential elements of the peace of the free world in the present international situation. Accordingly they will maintain armed forces within the territory of Berlin as long as their responsibilities require it. They therefore reaffirm that they will treat any attack against Berlin from any quarter as an attack upon their forces and themselves.

6. They will regard as a threat to their own peace and safety any recourse to force which in violation of the principles of the United Nations Charter threatens the integrity and unity of the Atlantic Alliance or its defensive purposes. In the event of any such action, the three Governments, for their part, will consider the offending Government as having forfeited its rights to any guarantee and any military assistance provided for in the North Atlantic Treaty and its Protocols. They will act in accordance with Article 4 of the North Atlantic Treaty with a view to taking other measures which may be appropriate.

7. They will invite the association of other Member States of the North Atlantic Treaty Organisation with this Declaration.

Protocol to the North Atlantic Treaty on the Accession of the Federal Republic of Germany

Paris, 23 October 1954

The Parties to the North Atlantic Treaty signed at Washington on April 4, 1949, Being satisfied that the security of the North Atlantic area will be enhanced by the accession of the Federal Republic of Germany to that Treaty, and Having noted that the Federal Republic of Germany has, by a declaration dated October 3, 1954, accepted the obligations set forth in Article 2 of the Charter of the United Nations and has undertaken upon its accession to the North Atlantic Treaty to refrain from any action inconsistent with the strictly defensive character of that Treaty, and

Having further noted that all member governments have associated themselves with the declaration also made on October 3, 1954, by the Governments of the United States of America, the United Kingdom of Great Britain and Northern Ireland and the French Republic in connection with the aforesaid declaration of the Federal Republic of Germany, Agree as follows:

ARTICLE 1

Upon the entry into force of the present Protocol, the Government of the United States of America shall on behalf of all the Parties communicate to the Government of the Federal Republic of Germany an invitation to accede to the North Atlantic Treaty. Thereafter the Federal Republic of Germany shall become a Party to that Treaty on the date when it depositsits instruments of accession with the Government of the United States of America in accordance with Article 10 of the Treaty.

ARTICLE 2

The present Protocol shall enter into force, when
    a. each of the Parties to the North Atlantic Treaty has notified to the Government of the United States of America its acceptance thereof,
    b. all instruments of ratification of the Protocol modifying and completing the Brussels Treaty have been deposited with the Belgian Government, and

    c.   all instruments of ratification or approval of the Convention on the Presence of Foreign Forces in the Federal Republic of Germany have been deposited with the Government of the Federal Republic of Germany.

The Government of the United States of America shall inform the other Parties to the North Atlantic Treaty of the date of the receipt of each notification of acceptance of the present Protocol and of the date of the entry into force of the present Protocol.

ARTICLE 3

The present Protocol, of which the English and French texts are equally authentic, shall be deposited in the Archives of the Government of the United States of America. Duly certified copies thereof shall be transmitted by that Government to the Governments of the other Parties to the North Atlantic Treaty.

Protocol to the North Atlantic Treaty on the Accession of Spain

The Parties to the North Atlantic Treaty,
signed at Washington on April 4, 1949,
Being satisfied that the security of the North Atlantic area will be
enhanced by the accession of the Kingdom of Spain to that Treaty,
Agree as follows:

Article 1

Upon the entry into force of this Protocol, the Secretary General of the North Atlantic Treaty Organization shall, on behalf of all the Parties, communicate to the Government of the Kingdom of Spain an invitation to accede to the North Atlantic Treaty. In accordance with Article 10 of the Treaty, the Kingdom of Spain shall become a Party on the date when it deposits its instrument of accession with the Government of the United States of America.

Article 2

The present Protocol shall enter into force when each of the Parties to the North Atlantic Treaty has notified the Government of the United States of America of its acceptance thereof. The Government of the United States of America shall inform all the Parties to the North Atlantic Treaty of the date of receipt of each such notification and of the date of the entry into force of the present Protocol.

Article 3

The present Protocol, of which the English and French texts are equally authentic, shall be deposited in the Archives of the Government of the United States of America. Duly certified copies thereof shall be transmitted by that Government to the Governments of all the Parties to the North Atlantic Treaty.

Protocol to the North Atlantic Treaty on the Accession of the Czech Republic

The Parties to the North Atlantic Treaty, signed at Washington on April 4, 1949,

Being satisfied that the security of the North Atlantic area will be enhanced by the accession of the Czech Republic to that Treaty,

Agree as follows:

Article I

Upon the entry into force of this Protocol, the Secretary General of the North Atlantic Treaty Organization shall, on behalf of all the Parties, communicate to the Government of the Czech Republic an invitation to accede to the North Atlantic Treaty. In accordance with article 10 of the Treaty, the Czech Republic shall become a Party on the date when it deposits its instrument of accession with the Government of the United States of America.

Article II

The present Protocol shall enter into force when each of the Parties to the North Atlantic Treaty has notified the Government of the United States of America of its acceptance thereof. The Government of the United States of America shall inform all the Parties to the North Atlantic Treaty of the date of receipt of each such notification and of the date of the entry into force of the present Protocol.

Article III

The present Protocol, of which the English and French texts are equally authentic, shall be deposited in the Archives of the Government of the United States of America. Duly certified copies thereof shall be transmitted by that Government to the Governments of all the Parties to the North Atlantic Treaty.

In witness whereof, the undersigned plenipotentiaries have signed the present Protocol.
Signed at Brussels on the 16th day of December 1997.

Protocol to the North Atlantic Treaty on the Accession of the Republic of Hungary

The Parties to the North Atlantic Treaty, signed at Washington on April 4, 1949,

Being satisfied that the security of the North Atlantic area will be enhanced by the accession of the Republic of Hungary to that Treaty,

Agree as follows:

Article I

Upon the entry into force of this Protocol, the Secretary General of the North Atlantic Treaty Organization shall, on behalf of all the Parties, communicate to the Government of the Republic of Hungary an invitation to accede to the North Atlantic Treaty. In accordance with article 10 of the Treaty, the Republic of Hungary shall become a Party on the date when it deposits its instrument of accession with the Government of the United States of America.

Article II

The present Protocol shall enter into force when each of the Parties to the North Atlantic Treaty has notified the Government of the United States of America of its acceptance thereof. The Government of the United States of America shall inform all the Parties to the North Atlantic Treaty of the date of receipt of each such notification and of the date of the entry into force of the present Protocol.

Article III

The present Protocol, of which the English and French texts are equally authentic, shall be deposited in the Archives of the Government of the United States of America. Duly certified copies thereof shall be transmitted by that Government to the Governments of all the Parties to the North Atlantic Treaty.

In witness whereof, the undersigned plenipotentiaries have signed the present Protocol.
Signed at Brussels on the 16th day of December 1997.

Protocol to the North Atlantic Treaty on the Accession of the Republic of Poland

The Parties to the North Atlantic Treaty, signed at Washington on April 4, 1949,

Being satisfied that the security of the North Atlantic area will be enhanced by the accession of the Republic of Poland to that Treaty,

Agree as follows:

Article I

Upon the entry into force of this Protocol, the Secretary General of the North Atlantic Treaty Organization shall, on behalf of all the Parties, communicate to the Government of the Republic of Poland an invitation to accede to the North Atlantic Treaty. In accordance with article 10 of the Treaty, the Republic of Poland shall become a Party on the date when it deposits its instrument of accession with the Government of the United States of America.

Article II

The present Protocol shall enter into force when each of the Parties to the North Atlantic Treaty has notified the Government of the United States of America of its acceptance thereof. The Government of the United States of America shall inform all the Parties to the North Atlantic Treaty of the date of receipt of each such notification and of the date of the entry into force of the present Protocol.

Article III

The present Protocol, of which the English and French texts are equally authentic, shall be deposited in the Archives of the Government of the United States of America. Duly certified copies thereof shall be transmitted by that Government to the Governments of all the Parties to the North Atlantic Treaty.

In witness whereof, the undersigned plenipotentiaries have signed the present Protocol.
Signed at Brussels on the 16th day of December 1997.

Protocol to the North Atlantic Treaty on the Accession of the Republic of Bulgaria

The Parties to the North Atlantic Treaty, signed at Washington on April 4, 1949,

Being satisfied that the security of the North Atlantic area will be enhanced by the accession of the Republic of Bulgaria to that Treaty,

Agree as follows:

Article I

Upon the entry into force of this Protocol, the Secretary General of the North Atlantic Treaty Organisation shall, on behalf of all the Parties, communicate to the Government of the Republic of Bulgaria an invitation to accede to the North Atlantic Treaty. In accordance with Article 10 of the Treaty, the Republic of Bulgaria shall become a Party on the date when it deposits its instrument of accession with the Government of the United States of America.

Article II

The present Protocol shall enter into force when each of the Parties to the North Atlantic Treaty has notified the Government of the United States of America of its acceptance thereof. The Government of the United States of America shall inform all the Parties to the North Atlantic Treaty of the date of receipt of each such notification and of the date of the entry into force of the present Protocol.

Article III

The present Protocol, of which the English and French texts are equally authentic, shall be deposited in the Archives of the Government of the United States of America. Duly certified copies thereof shall be transmitted by that Government to the Governments of all the Parties to the North Atlantic Treaty.

In witness whereof, the undersigned plenipotentiaries have signed the present Protocol.

Signed at Brussels on the 26th day of March 2003.

Protocol to the North Atlantic Treaty on the Accession of the Republic of Estonia

The Parties to the North Atlantic Treaty, signed at Washington on April 4, 1949,

Being satisfied that the security of the North Atlantic area will be enhanced by the accession of the Republic of Estonia to that Treaty,

Agree as follows:

Article I

Upon the entry into force of this Protocol, the Secretary General of the North Atlantic Treaty Organisation shall, on behalf of all the Parties, communicate to the Government of the Republic of Estonia an invitation to accede to the North Atlantic Treaty. In accordance with Article 10 of the Treaty, the Republic of Estonia shall become a Party on the date when it deposits its instrument of accession with the Government of the United States of America.

Article II

The present Protocol shall enter into force when each of the Parties to the North Atlantic Treaty has notified the Government of the United States of America of its acceptance thereof. The Government of the United States of America shall inform all the Parties to the North Atlantic Treaty of the date of receipt of each such notification and of the date of the entry into force of the present Protocol.

Article III

The present Protocol, of which the English and French texts are equally authentic, shall be deposited in the Archives of the Government of the United States of America. Duly certified copies thereof shall be transmitted by that Government to the Governments of all the Parties to the North Atlantic Treaty.

In witness whereof, the undersigned plenipotentiaries have signed the present Protocol.

Signed at Brussels on the 26th day of March 2003.

Protocol to the North Atlantic Treaty on the Accession of the Republic of Latvia

The Parties to the North Atlantic Treaty, signed at Washington on April 4, 1949,

Being satisfied that the security of the North Atlantic area will be enhanced by the accession of the Republic of Latvia to that Treaty,

Agree as follows:

Article I

Upon the entry into force of this Protocol, the Secretary General of the North Atlantic Treaty Organisation shall, on behalf of all the Parties, communicate to the Government of the Republic of Latvia an invitation to accede to the North Atlantic Treaty. In accordance with Article 10 of the Treaty, the Republic of Latvia shall become a Party on the date when it deposits its instrument of accession with the Government of the United States of America.

Article II

The present Protocol shall enter into force when each of the Parties to the North Atlantic Treaty has notified the Government of the United States of America of its acceptance thereof. The Government of the United States of America shall inform all the Parties to the North Atlantic Treaty of the date of receipt of each such notification and of the date of the entry into force of the present Protocol.

Article III

The present Protocol, of which the English and French texts are equally authentic, shall be deposited in the Archives of the Government of the United States of America. Duly certified copies thereof shall be transmitted by that Government to the Governments of all the Parties to the North Atlantic Treaty.

In witness whereof, the undersigned plenipotentiaries have signed the present Protocol.

Signed at Brussels on the 26th day of March 2003.

Protocol to the North Atlantic Treaty on the Accession of the Republic of Lithuania

The Parties to the North Atlantic Treaty, signed at Washington on April 4, 1949,

Being satisfied that the security of the North Atlantic area will be enhanced by the accession of the Republic of Lithuania to that Treaty,

Agree as follows:

Article I

Upon the entry into force of this Protocol, the Secretary General of the North Atlantic Treaty Organisation shall, on behalf of all the Parties, communicate to the Government of the Republic of Lithuania an invitation to accede to the North Atlantic Treaty. In accordance with Article 10 of the Treaty, the Republic of Lithuania shall become a Party on the date when it deposits its instrument of accession with the Government of the United States of America.

Article II

The present Protocol shall enter into force when each of the Parties to the North Atlantic Treaty has notified the Government of the United States of America of its acceptance thereof. The Government of the United States of America shall inform all the Parties to the North Atlantic Treaty of the date of receipt of each such notification and of the date of the entry into force of the present Protocol.

Article III

The present Protocol, of which the English and French texts are equally authentic, shall be deposited in the Archives of the Government of the United States of America. Duly certified copies thereof shall be transmitted by that Government to the Governments of all the Parties to the North Atlantic Treaty.

In witness whereof, the undersigned plenipotentiaries have signed the present Protocol.

Signed at Brussels on the 26th day of March 2003.

Protocol to the North Atlantic Treaty on the Accession of Romania

The Parties to the North Atlantic Treaty, signed at Washington on April 4, 1949,

Being satisfied that the security of the North Atlantic area will be enhanced by the accession of Romania to that Treaty,

Agree as follows:

Article I

Upon the entry into force of this Protocol, the Secretary General of the North Atlantic Treaty Organisation shall, on behalf of all the Parties, communicate to the Government of Romania an invitation to accede to the North Atlantic Treaty. In accordance with Article 10 of the Treaty, Romania shall become a Party on the date when it deposits its instrument of accession with the Government of the United States of America.

Article II

The present Protocol shall enter into force when each of the Parties to the North Atlantic Treaty has notified the Government of the United States of America of its acceptance thereof. The Government of the United States of America shall inform all the Parties to the North Atlantic Treaty of the date of receipt of each such notification and of the date of the entry into force of the present Protocol.

Article III

The present Protocol, of which the English and French texts are equally authentic, shall be deposited in the Archives of the Government of the United States of America. Duly certified copies thereof shall be transmitted by that Government to the Governments of all the Parties to the North Atlantic Treaty.

In witness whereof, the undersigned plenipotentiaries have signed the present Protocol.

Signed at Brussels on the 26th day of March 2003.

Protocol to the North Atlantic Treaty on the Accession of the Slovak Republic

The Parties to the North Atlantic Treaty, signed at Washington on April 4, 1949,

Being satisfied that the security of the North Atlantic area will be enhanced by the accession of the Slovak Republic to that Treaty,

Agree as follows:

Article I

Upon the entry into force of this Protocol, the Secretary General of the North Atlantic Treaty Organisation shall, on behalf of all the Parties, communicate to the Government of the Slovak Republic an invitation to accede to the North Atlantic Treaty. In accordance with Article 10 of the Treaty, the Slovak Republic shall become a Party on the date when it deposits its instrument of accession with the Government of the United States of America.

Article II

The present Protocol shall enter into force when each of the Parties to the North Atlantic Treaty has notified the Government of the United States of America of its acceptance thereof. The Government of the United States of America shall inform all the Parties to the North Atlantic Treaty of the date of receipt of each such notification and of the date of the entry into force of the present Protocol.

Article III

The present Protocol, of which the English and French texts are equally authentic, shall be deposited in the Archives of the Government of the United States of America. Duly certified copies thereof shall be transmitted by that Government to the Governments of all the Parties to the North Atlantic Treaty.

In witness whereof, the undersigned plenipotentiaries have signed the present Protocol.

Signed at Brussels on the 26th day of March 2003.

Protocol to the North Atlantic Treaty on the Accession of the Republic of Slovenia

The Parties to the North Atlantic Treaty, signed at Washington on April 4, 1949,

Being satisfied that the security of the North Atlantic area will be enhanced by the accession of the Republic of Slovenia to that Treaty,

Agree as follows:

Article I

Upon the entry into force of this Protocol, the Secretary General of the North Atlantic Treaty Organisation shall, on behalf of all the Parties, communicate to the Government of the Republic of Slovenia an invitation to accede to the North Atlantic Treaty. In accordance with Article 10 of the Treaty, the Republic of Slovenia shall become a Party on the date when it deposits its instrument of accession with the Government of the United States of America.

Article II

The present Protocol shall enter into force when each of the Parties to the North Atlantic Treaty has notified the Government of the United States of America of its acceptance thereof. The Government of the United States of America shall inform all the Parties to the North Atlantic Treaty of the date of receipt of each such notification and of the date of the entry into force of the present Protocol.

Article III

The present Protocol, of which the English and French texts are equally authentic, shall be deposited in the Archives of the Government of the United States of America. Duly certified copies thereof shall be transmitted by that Government to the Governments of all the Parties to the North Atlantic Treaty.

In witness whereof, the undersigned plenipotentiaries have signed the present Protocol.

Signed at Brussels on the 26th day of March 2003.

Agreement
On the Status of the North Atlantic Treaty Organization, National Representatives And International Staff

The States signatory to the present Agreement, considering that for the exercise of their functions and the fulfilment of their purposes it is necessary that the North Atlantic Treaty Organization, its international staff and the representatives of Member States attending meetings thereof should have the status set out hereunder, Have agreed as follows:

Part I. General

Article I

In the present Agreement,

a. 'the Organization' means the North Atlantic Treaty Organization consisting of the Council and its subsidiary bodies;

b. 'the Council' means the Council established under Article IX of the North Atlantic Treaty and the Council Deputies;

c. 'subsidiary bodies' means any organ, committee or service established by the Council or under its authority, except those to which, in accordance with Article II, this Agreement does not apply;

d. 'Chairman of the Council Deputies' includes, in his absence, the Vice-Chairman acting for him.

Article II

The present Agreement shall not apply to any military headquarters established in pursuance of the North Atlantic Treaty nor, unless the Council decides otherwise, to any other military bodies.

Article III

The Organization and Member States shall co-operate at all times to facilitate the proper administration of justice, secure the observance of police regulations and prevent the occurrence of any abuse in connection with the immunities and privileges set out in the present Agreement. If any Member State considers that there has been an abuse of any immunity or privilege conferred by this Agreement, consultations shall be held between that State and the Organization, or between the States concerned, to determine whether any such abuse has occurred, and, if so, to attempt to ensure hat no repetition occurs. Notwithstanding the foregoing or any other provisions of this Agreement, a Member State which considers that any person has abused his privilege of residence or any other privilege or immunity granted to him under this Agreement may require him to leave its territory.

Part II. The Organization

Article IV
The Organization shall possess juridical personality; it shall have the capacity to conclude contracts, to acquire and dispose of movable and immovable property and to institute legal proceedings.

Article V
The Organization, its property and assets, wheresoever located and by whomsoever held, shall enjoy immunity from every form of legal process except in so far as in any particular case the Chairman of the Council Deputies, acting on behalf of the Organization, may expressly authorize the waiver of this immunity. It is however, understood that no waiver of immunity shall extend to any measure of execution or detention of property.

Article VI
The premises of the Organization shall be inviolable. Its property and assets, wheresoever located and by whomsoever held, shall be immune from search, requisition, confiscation, expropriation or any other form of interference.

Article VII
The archives of the Organization and all documents belonging to it or held by it shall be inviolable, wherever located.

Article VIII
1. Without being restricted by financial controls, regulations or moratoria of any kind,
    a. the Organization may hold currency of any kind and operate accounts in any currency;
    b. the Organization may freely transfer its funds from one country to another or within any country and convert any currency held by it into any other currency at the most favourable official rate of exchange for a sale or purchase as the case may be.

2. In exercising its rights under paragraph 1 above, the Organization shall pay due regard to any representations made by any Member State and shall give effect to such representations in so far as it is practicable to do so.

Article IX

The Organization, its assets, income and other property shall be exempt:

a. from all direct taxes; the Organization will not, however, claim exemption from rates, taxes or dues which are no more than charges for public utility services;

b. from all customs duties and quantitative restrictions on imports and exports in respect of articles imported or exported by the Organization for its official use; articles imported under such exemption shall not be disposed of, by way either of sale or gift, in the country into which they are imported except under conditions approved by the Government of that country;

c. from all customs duties and quantitative restrictions on imports and exports in respect of its publications.

Article X

While the Organization will not as a general rule claim exemption from excise duties and from taxes on the sale of movable and immovable property which form part of the price to be paid, nevertheless, when the Organization is making important purchases for official use of property on which such duties and taxes have been charged or are chargeable, Member States will whenever possible make the appropriate administrative arrangements for the remission or return of the amount of duty or tax.

Article XI

1. No censorship shall be applied to the official correspondence and other official communications of the Organization.

2. The Organization shall have the right to use codes and to despatch and receive correspondence by courier or in sealed bags, which shall have the same immunities and privileges as diplomatic couriers and bags.

3. Nothing in this Article shall be construed to preclude the adoption of appropriate security precautions to be determined by agreement between a Member State and the Council acting on behalf of the Organization.

Part III. Representatives Of Member States

Article XII

Every person designated by a Member State as its principal permanent representative to the Organization in the territory of another Member State, and such members of his official staff resident in that territory as may be agreed between the State which has designated them and the Organization and between the Organization and the State in which they will be resident, shall enjoy the immunities and privileges accorded to diplomatic representatives and their official staff of comparable rank.

Article XIII

1. Any representative of a Member State to the Council or any of its subsidiary bodies who is not covered by Article XII shall, while present in the territory of another Member State for the discharge of his duties, enjoy the following privileges and immunities:
    a. the same immunity from personal arrest or detention as that accorded to diplomatic personnel of comparable rank;
    b. in respect of words spoken or written and of acts done by him in his official capacity, immunity from legal process;
    c. inviolability for all papers and documents;
    d. the right to use codes and to receive and send papers or correspondence by courier or in sealed bags;
    e. the same exemption in respect of himself and his spouse from immigration restrictions, aliens registration and national service obligations as that accorded to diplomatic personnel of comparable rank;
    f. the same facilities in respect of currency or exchange restrictions as are accorded to diplomatic personnel of comparable rank;
    g. the same immunities and facilities in respect of his personal baggage as are accorded to diplomatic personnel of comparable rank;
    h. the right to import free of duty his furniture and effects at the time of first arrival to take up his post in the country in question, and, on the termination of his functions in that country, to re-export such furniture and effects free of duty, subject in either case to such conditions as the Government of the country in which the right is being exercised may deem necessary;
    i. the right to import temporarily free of duty his private motor vehicle for his own personal use and subsequently to re-export such vehicle

free or duty, subject in either case to such conditions as the Government of the country concerned may deem necessary.

2. Where the Legal incidence of any form of taxation depends upon residence, a period during which a representative to whom this Article applies is present in the territory of another Member State for the discharge of his duties shall not be considered as a period of residence. In particular, he shall he exempt from taxation on his official salary and emoluments during such periods of duty.

3. In this Article 'representative' shall be deemed to include all representatives, advisers and technical experts of delegations. Each Member State shall communicate to the other Member States concerned, if they so request, the names of its representatives to whom this Article applies and the probable duration of their stay in the territories of such other Member States.

Article XIV

Official clerical staff accompanying a representative of a Member State who are not covered by Articles XII or XIII shall, while present in the territory of another Member State for the discharge of their duties, be accorded the privileges and immunities set out in paragraph 1 b., c., e., f., h. and i., and paragraph 2 of Article XIII.

Article XV

Privileges and immunities are accorded to the representatives of Member States and their staffs not for the personal benefit of the individuals themselves, but in order to safeguard the independent exercise of their functions in connection with the North Atlantic Treaty. Consequently, a Member State not only has the right but is under a duty to waive the immunity of its representatives and members of their staffs in any case where, in its opinion, the immunity would impede the course of justice and can be waived without prejudice to the purposes for which the immunity is accorded.

Article XVI

The provisions of Articles XII to XIV above shall not require any State to grant any of the privileges or immunities referred to therein to any person who is its national or to any person as its representative or as a member of the staff of such representative.

Part IV. International Staff and Experts on Missions for the Organization

Article XVII
The categories of officials of the Organization to which Articles XVIII to XX apply shall be agreed between the Chairman of the Council Deputies and each of the Member States concerned. The Chairman of the Council Deputies shall communicate to the Member States the names of the officials included in these categories.

Article XVIII
Officials of the Organization agreed upon under Article XVII shall:
    a. be immune from legal process in respect of words spoken or written and of acts done by them in their official capacity and within the limits of their authority;
    b. be granted, together with their spouses and members of their immediate families residing with and dependent on them, the same immunities from immigration restrictions and aliens' registration as is accorded to diplomatic personnel of comparable rank;
    c. be accorded the same facilities in respect of currency or exchange restrictions as are accorded to diplomatic personnel of comparable rank;
    d. be given, together with their spouses and members of their immediate families residing with and dependent on them, the same repatriation facilities in time of international crisis as are accorded to diplomatic personnel of comparable rank;
    e. have the right to import free of duty their furniture and effects at the time of first arrival to take up their post in the country in question, and, on the termination of their functions in that country, to re-export such furniture and effects free of duty, subject in either case to such conditions as the Government of the country in which the right is being exercised may deem necessary;
    f. have the right to import temporarily free of duty their private motor vehicles for their own personal use and subsequently to re-export such vehicles free of duty, subject in either case to such conditions as the Government of the country concerned may deem necessary.

Article XIX
Officials of the Organization agreed under Article XVII shall be exempt from taxation on the salaries and emoluments paid to them by the Organization in their capacity as such officials. Any Member State may, however, conclude an

arrangement with the Council acting on behalf of the Organization whereby such Member State will employ and assign to the Organization all of its nationals (except, if such Member State so desires, any not ordinarily resident within its territory) who are to serve on the international staff of the Organization and pay the salaries and emoluments of such persons from its own funds at a scale fixed by it. The salaries and emoluments so paid may be taxed by such Member State but shall be exempt from taxation by any other Member State. If such an arrangement is entered into by any Member State and is subsequently modified or terminated, Member States shall no longer be bound under the first sentence of this Article to exempt from taxation the salaries and emoluments paid to their nationals.

In addition to the immunities and privileges specified in Articles XVIII and XIX, the Executive Secretary of the Organization, the Co-ordinator of North Atlantic Defence Production, and such other permanent officials of similar rank as may be agreed between the Chairman of the Council Deputies and the Governments of Member States, shall be accorded the privileges and immunities normally accorded to diplomatic personnel of comparable rank.

Article XX

In addition to the immunities and privileges specified in Articles XVIII and XIX, the Executive Secretary of the Organisation, the Coordinator of North Atlantic Defence Production, and such other permanent officials of similar rank as may be agreed between the Chairman of the Council Deputies and the Governments of Member States, shall be accorded the privileges and immunities normally accorded to diplomatic personnel of comparable rank.

Article XXI

1. Experts (other than officials coming within the scope of Articles XVIII to XX) employed on missions on behalf of the Organization shall be accorded the following privileges and immunities so far as is necessary for the effective exercise of their functions while present in the territory of a Member State for the discharge of their duties:
   a. immunity from personal arrest or detention and from seizure of their personal baggage;
   b. in respect of words spoken or written or acts done by them in the performance of their official functions for the Organization, immunity from legal process;
   c. the same facilities in respect of currency or exchange restrictions and in respect of their personal baggage as are accorded to officials of foreign Governments on temporary official missions;

    d. inviolability for all papers and documents relating to the work on which they are engaged for the Organization.

2. The Chairman of the Council Deputies shall communicate to the Member States concerned the names of any experts to whom this Article applies.

Article XXII

Privileges and immunities are granted to officials and experts in the interests of the Organization and not for the personal benefit of the individuals themselves. The Chairman of the Council Deputies shall have the right and the duty to waive the immunity of any official or expert in any case where, in his opinion, the immunity would impede the course of justice and can be waived without prejudice to the interests of the Organization.

Article XXIII

The provisions of Articles XVIII, XX and XXI above shall not require any State to grant any of the privileges or immunities referred to therein to any person who is its national, except:

    a. immunity from legal process in respect of words spoken or written or acts done by him in the performance of his official functions for the Organization;

    b. inviolability for all papers and documents relating to the work on which he is engaged for the Organization;

    c. facilities in respect of currency or exchange restrictions so far as necessary for the effective exercise of his functions.

Part V. Settlement of Disputes

Article XXIV

The Council shall make provision for appropriate modes of settlement of:

    a. disputes arising out of contracts or other disputes of a private character to which the Organization is a party;

    b. disputes involving any official or expert of the Organization to whom Part IV of this Agreement applies who by reason of his official position enjoys immunity; if immunity has not been waived in accordance with the provisions of Article XXII.

Part VI. Supplementary Agreements

Article XXV

The Council acting on behalf of the Organization may conclude with any Member State or States supplementary agreements modifying the provisions of the present Agreement, so far as that State or those States are concerned.

Part VII. Final Provisions

Article XXVI

1. The present Agreement shall be open for signature by Member States of the Organization and shall be subject to ratification. Instruments of ratification shall be deposited with the Government of the United States of America, which will notify all signatory States of each such deposit.
2. As soon as six signatory States have deposited their instruments of ratification, the present Agreement shall come into force in respect of those States. It shall come into force in respect of each other signatory State on the date of the deposit of its instrument of ratification.

Article XXVII

The present Agreement may be denounced by any Contracting State by giving written notification of denunciation to the Government of the United States of America, which will notify all signatory States of each such notification. The denunciation shall take effect one year after the receipt of the notification by the Government of the United States of America.

In witness whereof the undersigned plenipotentiaries have signed the present Agreement. Done in Ottawa this twentieth day of September, 1951, in French and in English, both texts being equally authoritative, in a single copy which shall be deposited in the archives of the Government of the United States of America which will transmit a certified copy to each of the signatory States.

Agreement
on the Status of Missions and
Representatives of Third States to the North
Atlantic Treaty Organization

Considering the Declaration on Peace and Cooperation issued by the
Heads of State and Government participating in the meeting of the
North Atlantic Council in Rome on 7th and 8th November 1991
calling for the establishment of a North Atlantic Cooperation
Council and the North Atlantic Cooperation Council Statement on
Dialogue, Partnership and Cooperation of 20th December 1991;

Noting the Partnership for Peace invitation issued and signed by the Heads of
State and Government of the member States of the North Atlantic Treaty
Organization at the meeting of the North Atlantic Council in Brussels on 10th
January 1994;

Recognizing the need to determine the status of the missions and representatives
of third States to the Organization;

Considering that the purpose of immunities and privileges contained in the present Agreement is not to benefit individuals but to ensure the efficient performance of their function in connection with the Organization;

The Parties to the present Agreement have agreed as follows:

Article 1:

For the purpose of the present Agreement:

"Organization" means: The North Atlantic Treaty Organization;

"Member State" means: A State Party to the North Atlantic Treaty done in
Washington on 4th April 1949;

"Third State" means: A State which is not a Party to the North Atlantic Treaty
done in Washington on 4th April 1949, and which has accepted the invitation
to the Partnership for Peace and subscribed to the Partnership for Peace

Framework Document, is a member State of the North Atlantic Cooperation Council or is any other State invited by the North Atlantic Council to establish a Mission to the Organization.

Article 2:

a.   The member State in whose territory the Organization has its headquarters shall accord to the missions of third States to the Organization and the members of their Staff the immunities and privileges accorded to diplomatic missions and their staff;

b.   In addition, the member State in whose territory the Organization has its headquarters shall accord the customary immunities and privileges to the representatives of third States, on temporary mission, who are not covered by paragraph (a) of the present Article, while present in its territory for the purpose of ensuring the representation of third States in relation to the proceedings of the Organization.

Article 3:

a.   The present Agreement shall be open for signature by member States and shall be subject to ratification, acceptance or approval. Instruments of ratification, acceptance or approval shall be deposited with the Government of the Kingdom of Belgium which shall notify all signatory States of the deposit of each such instrument;

b.   As soon as two or more signatory States, including the member State in whose territory the Organization has its headquarters, have deposited their instruments of ratification, acceptance or approval, the present Agreement shall come into force in respect of those States. It shall come into force in respect of each other signatory State on the date of the deposit of its instrument.

Article 4:

a.   The present Agreement may be denounced by any contracting State by giving written notification of denunciation of the Government of the Kingdom of Belgium which shall notify all signatory States of each such notification;

b.   The denunciation shall take effect one year after the receipt of the notification by the Government of the Kingdom of Belgium.

In witness whereof the undersigned, being duly authorised by their respective Governments, have signed the present Agreement of which the English and French texts are equally authentic.

Done in Brussels, this 14th Day of September 1994.

Agreement
Between the Parties to the North Atlantic
Treaty Regarding the Status of Their Forces

The parties to the North Atlantic Treaty signed in Washington on 4 April, 1949, Considering that the forces of one Party may be sent, by arrangement, to serve in the territory of another Party;

Bearing in mind that the decision to send them and the conditions under which they will be sent, in so far as such conditions are not laid down by the present Agreement, will continue to be the subject of separate arrangements between the Parties concerned;

Desiring, however, to define the status of such forces while in the territory of another Party; Have agreed as follows:

Article I
1. In this Agreement the expression
    a. 'force' means the personnel belonging to the land, sea or air armed services of one Contracting Party when in the territory of another Contracting Party in the North Atlantic Treaty area in connexion with their official duties, provided that the two Contracting Parties concerned may agree that certain individuals, units or formations shall not be regarded as constituting or included in a 'force' for the purpose of the present Agreement;
    b. 'civilian component' means the civilian personnel accompanying a force of a Contracting Party who are in the employ of an armed service of that Contracting Party, and who are not stateless persons, nor nationals of any State which is not a Party to the North Atlantic Treaty, nor nationals of, nor ordinarily resident in, the State in which the force is located.
    c. 'dependent' means the spouse of a member of a force or a civilian component, or a child of such member depending on him or her for support;
    d. 'sending State' means the Contracting Party to which the force belongs;

42

e. 'receiving State' means the Contracting Party in the territory of which the force or civilian component is located, whether it be stationed there or passing in transit;

f. 'military authorities of the sending State' means those authorities of a sending State who are empowered by its law to enforce the military law of that State with respect to members of its forces or civilian components;

g. 'North Atlantic Council' means the Council established by Article 9 of the North Atlantic Treaty or any of its subsidiary bodies authorised to act on its behalf.

2. This Agreement shall apply to the authorities of political sub-divisions of the Contracting Parties, within their territories to which the Agreement applies or extends in accordance with Article XX, as it applies to the central authorities of those Contracting Parties, provided, however, that property owned by political sub-divisions shall not be considered to be property owned by a Contracting Party within the meaning of Article VIII.

Article II

It is the duty of a force and its civilian component and the members thereof as well as their dependents to respect the law of the receiving State, and to abstain from any activity inconsistent with the spirit of the present Agreement, and, in particular, from any political activity in the receiving State. It is also the duty of the sending State to take necessary of measures to that end.

Article III

1. On the conditions specified in paragraph 2 of this Article and subject to compliance with the formalities established by the receiving State relating to entry and departure of a force or the members thereof, such members shall be exempt from passport and visa regulations and immigration inspection on entering or leaving the territory of a receiving State. They shall also be exempt from the regulations of the receiving State on the registration and control of aliens, but shall not be considered as acquiring any right to permanent residence or domicile in the territories of the receiving State

2. The following documents only will be required in respect of members of a force. They must be presented on demand:

a. personal identity card issued by the sending State showing names, date of birth, rank and number (if any), service, and photograph;

    b.   individual or collective movement order, in the language of the sending State and in the English and French languages, issued by an appropriate agency of the sending State or of the North Atlantic Treaty Organization and certifying to the status of the individual or group as a member or members of a force and to the movement ordered. The receiving State may require a movement order to be countersigned by its appropriate representative.

3.   Members of a civilian component and dependents shall be so described in their passports.

4.   If a member of a force or a civilian component leaves the employ of the sending State and is not repatriated, the authorities of the sending State shall immediately inform the authorities of the receiving State, giving such particulars as may be required. The authorities of the sending State shall similarly inform the authorities of the receiving State of any member who has absented himself for more than twenty-one days.

5.   If the receiving State has requested the removal from its territory of a member of a force or civilian component or has made an expulsion order against an ex-member of a force or of a civilian component or against a dependent of a member or ex-member, the authorities of the sending State shall be responsible for receiving the person concerned within their own territory or otherwise disposing of him outside the receiving State. This paragraph shall apply only to persons who are not nationals of the receiving State and have entered the receiving State as members of a force or civilian component or for the purpose of becoming such members, and to the dependents of such persons.

Article IV

The receiving State shall either

    a.   accept as valid, without a driving test or fee, the driving permit or licence or military driving permit issued by the sending State or a sub-division thereof to a member of a force or of a civilian component; or

    b.   issue its own driving permit or licence to any member of a force or civilian component who holds a driving permit or licence or military driving permit issued by the sending State or a sub-division thereof, provided that no driving test shall be required.

Article V

1.   Members of a force shall normally wear uniform. Subject to any arrangement to the contrary between the authorities of the sending and receiving States, the wearing of civilian dress shall be on the same conditions as for

members of the forces of the receiving State. Regularly constituted units or formations of a force shall be in uniform when crossing a frontier.

2. Service vehicles of a force or civilian component shall carry, in addition to their registration number, a distinctive nationality mark.

Article VI

Members of a force may possess and carry arms, on condition that they are authorized to do so by their orders. The authorities of the sending State shall give sympathetic consideration to requests from the receiving State concerning this matter.

Article VII

1. Subject to the provisions of this Article,
   a. the military authorities of the sending State shall have the right to exercise within the receiving State all criminal and disciplinary jurisdiction conferred on them by the law of the sending State over all persons subject to the military law of that State;
   b. the authorities of the receiving State shall have jurisdiction over the members of a force or civilian component and their dependents with respect to offences committed within the territory of the receiving State and punishable by the law of that State.

2.
   a. The military authorities of the sending State shall have the right to exercise exclusive jurisdiction over persons subject to the military law of that State with respect to offences, including offences relating to its security, punishable by the law of the sending State, but not by the law of the receiving State.
   b. The authorities of the receiving State shall have the right to exercise exclusive jurisdiction over members of a force or civilian component and their dependents with respect to offences, including offences relating to the security of that State, punishable by its law but not by the law of the sending state.
   c. For the purposes of this paragraph and of paragraph 3 of this Article a security offence against a State shall include:
      i. treason against the State;
      ii. sabotage, espionage or violation of any law relating to official secrets of that State, or secrets relating to the national defence of that State

3. In case where the right to exercise jurisdiction is concurrent the following rules shall apply:

    a. The military authorities of the sending State shall have the primary right to exercise jurisdiction over a member of a force or of a civilian component in relation to

        i. offences solely against the property or security of that State, or offences solely against the person or property of another member of the force or civilian component of that State or of a dependent;

        ii. offences arising out of any act or omission done in the performance of official duty.

    b. In the case of any other offence the authorities of the receiving State shall have the primary right to exercise jurisdiction.

    c. If the State having the primary right decides not to exercise jurisdiction, it shall notify the authorities of the other State as soon as practicable. The authorities of the State having the primary right shall give sympathetic consideration to a request from the authorities of the other State for a waiver of its right in cases where that other state considers such waiver to be of particular importance.

4. The foregoing provisions of this Article shall not imply any right for the military authorities of the sending State to exercise jurisdiction over persons who are nationals of or ordinarily resident in the receiving State, unless they are members of the force of the sending State.

5.

    a. The authorities of the receiving and sending states shall assist each other in the arrest of members of a force or civilian component or their dependents in the territory of the receiving State and in handing them over to the authority which is to exercise jurisdiction in accordance with the above provisions.

    b. The authorities of the receiving State shall notify promptly the military authorities of the sending State of the arrest of any member of a force or civilian component or a dependent.

    c. The custody of an accused member of a force or civilian component over whom the receiving state is to exercise jurisdiction shall, if he is in the hands of the sending State, remain with that State until he is charged by the receiving State.

6.

    a. The authorities of the receiving and sending States shall assist each other in the carrying out of all necessary investigations into offences, and in the collection and production of evidence, including the seizure and, in proper cases, the handing over of objects connected with an offence. The handing over of such objects may, however, be made subject to their return within the time specified by the authority delivering them.

b. The authorities of the Contracting parties shall notify one another of the disposition of all cases in which there are concurrent rights to exercise jurisdiction.

7.

a. A death sentence shall not be carried out in the receiving State by the authorities of the sending State if the legislation of the receiving state does not provide for such punishment in a similar case.

b. The authorities of the receiving State shall give sympathetic consideration to a request from the authorities of the sending State for assistance in carrying out a sentence of imprisonment pronounced by the authorities of the sending State under the provision of this Article within the territory of the receiving State.

8. Where an accused has been tried in accordance with the provisions of this Article by the authorities of one Contracting Party and has been acquitted, or has been convicted and is serving, or has served, his sentence or has been pardoned, he may not be tried again for the same offence within the same territory by the authorities of another Contracting Party. However, nothing in this paragraph shall prevent the military authorities of the sending State from trying a member of its force for any violation of rules of discipline arising from an act or omission which constituted an offence for which he was tried by the authorities of another Contracting Party.

9. Whenever a member of a force or civilian component of a dependent is prosecuted under the jurisdiction of a receiving State he shall be entitled:

a. to a prompt and speedy trial;

b. to be informed, in advance of trial, of the specific charge or charges made against him;

c. to be confronted with the witnesses against him;

d. to have compulsory process for obtaining witnesses in his favour, if they are within the jurisdiction of the receiving State;

e. to have legal representation of his own choice for his defence or to have free or assisted legal representation under the conditions prevailing for the time being in the receiving State;

f. if he considers it necessary, to have the services of a competent interpreter; and

g.   to communicate with a representative of the Government of the sending State and when the rules of the court permit, to have such a representative present at his trial.

10.

a.   Regularly constituted military units or formations of a force shall have the right to police any camps, establishment or other premises which they occupy as the result of an agreement with the receiving State. The military police of the force may take all appropriate measures to ensure the maintenance of order and security on such premises.

b.   Outside these premises, such military police shall be employed only subject to arrangements with the authorities of the receiving State and in liaison with those authorities, and in so far as such employment is necessary to maintain discipline and order among the members of the force.

11.   Each Contracting Party shall seek such legislation as it deems necessary to ensure the adequate security and protection within its territory of installations, equipment, property, records and official information of other Contracting Parties, and the punishment of persons who may contravene laws enacted for that purpose.

Article VIII

1.   Each Contracting Party waives all its claims against any other Contracting Party for damage to any property owned by it and used by its land; sea or air armed services, if such damage:

i.   was caused by a member or an employee of the armed services of the other Contracting Party in the execution of his duties in connection with the operation of the North Atlantic Treaty; or

ii.   arose from the use of any vehicle, vessel or aircraft owned by the other Contracting Party and used by its armed services, provided either that the vehicle, vessel or aircraft causing the damage was being used in connection with the operation of the North Atlantic Treaty, or that the damage was caused to property being so used.

Claims for maritime salvage by one Contracting Party against any other Contracting Party shall be waived, provided that the vessel or cargo salvaged was owned by a contracting Party and being used by its armed services in connection with the operation of the North Atlantic Treaty.

2.

i.   In the case of damage caused or arising as stated in paragraph 1 to other property owned by a Contracting Party and located in its territory, the issue of the liability of any other Contracting Party shall be determined and the amount of damage shall be assessed, unless the Contracting Parties concerned agree otherwise, by a sole arbitrator selected in accordance with sub-paragraph b. of this paragraph. The arbitrator shall also decide any counter-claims arising out of the same incident.

ii. The arbitrator referred to in sub-paragraph a. above shall be selected by agreement between the Contracting Parties concerned from amongst the nationals of the receiving State who hold or have held high judicial office. If the Contracting Parties concerned are unable, within two months, to agree upon the arbitrator, either may request the Chairman of the North Atlantic Council Deputies to select a person with the aforesaid qualifications.

iii. Any decision taken by the arbitrator shall be binding and conclusive upon the Contracting Parties.

iv. The amount of any compensation awarded by the arbitrator shall be distributed in accordance with the provisions of paragraph 5 e. (i), (ii) and (iii) of this Article.

v. The compensation of the arbitrator shall be fixed by agreement between the Contracting Parties concerned and shall, together with the necessary expenses incidental to performance of his duties, be defrayed in equal proportions by them.

vi. Nevertheless, each Contracting Party waives its claim in any such case where the damage is less than:

Belgium:	B. fr. 70,000.	Luxembourg:	L. fr. 70,000.
Canada:	$ 1,460.	Netherlands:	Fl. 5,320
Denmark:	Kr. 9,670.	Norway:	Kr. 10,000.
France:	F. fr. 490,000.	Portugal:	Es. 40,250.
Iceland:	Kr. 22,800.	United Kingdom:	£ 500.
Italy:	Li. 850,000.	United States:	$ 1,400.

vii. Any other Contracting Party whose property has been damaged in the same incident shall also waive its claim up to the above amount. In the case of considerable variation in the rates of exchange between these currencies the Contracting Parties shall agree on the appropriate adjustments of these amounts.

- For the purposes of paragraphs 1 and 2 of this Article the expression "owned by a Contacting Party" in the case of a vessel includes a vessel on bare boat charter to that Contracting Party or requisitioned by it on bare boat terms or seized by it in prize (except to the extent that the risk of loss or liability is borne by some person other than such Contracting Party).

- Each Contracting Party waives all its claims against any other Contracting Party for injury or death suffered by any member of its armed services while such member was engaged in the performance of his official duties.

- Claims (other than contractual claims and those to which paragraphs 6 or 7 of this Article apply) arising out of acts or omissions of members of a force or civilian component done in the performance of official duty, or out of any other act, omission or occurrence for which a force or civilian component is legally responsible, and causing damage in the territory of the receiving State to third parties, other than any of the Contracting Parties, shall be dealt with by the receiving State in accordance with the following provisions:

i. Claims shall be filed, considered and settled or adjudicated in accordance with the laws and regulations of the receiving State with respect to claims arising from the activities of its own armed forces.

ii. The receiving State may settle any such claims, and payment of the amount agreed upon or determined by adjudication shall be made by the receiving State in its currency.

iii. Such payment, whether made pursuant to a settlement or to adjudication of the case by a competent tribunal of the receiving State, or the final adjudication by such a tribunal denying payment, shall be binding and conclusive upon the Contracting Parties.

iv. Every claim paid by the receiving State shall be communicated to the sending States concerned together with full particulars and a proposed distribution in conformity with sub-paragraphs e. (i), (ii) and (iii) below. In default of a reply within two months, the proposed distribution shall be regarded as accepted.

v. The cost incurred in satisfying claims pursuant to the preceding sub-paragraphs and para. 2 of this Article shall be distributed between the Contracting Parties, as follows:

i. Where one sending State alone is responsible, the amount awarded or adjudged shall be distributed in the proportion of 25 per cent. chargeable to the receiving State and 75 per cent. chargeable to the sending State.

ii. Where more than one State is responsible for the damage, the amount awarded or adjudged shall be distributed equally among them: however, if the receiving State is not one of the States responsible, its contribution shall be half that of each of the sending States.

iii. Where the damage was caused by the armed services of the Contracting Parties and it is not possible to attribute it specifically to one or more of those armed services, the amount awarded or adjudged shall be distributed equally among the Contracting Parties concerned: however, if the receiving State is not one of the States by whose armed services the damage was caused, its contribution shall be half that of each of the sending States concerned.

iv. Every half-year, a statement of the sums paid by the receiving State in the course of the half-yearly period in respect of every case regarding which the proposed distribution on a percentage basis has been accepted, shall be sent to the sending States concerned, together with a request for reimbursement. Such reimbursement shall be made within the shortest possible time, in the currency of the receiving State.

vi. In cases where the application of the provisions of sub-paragraphs b. and e. of this paragraph would cause a Contracting Party serious hardship, it may request the North Atlantic Council to arrange a settlement of a different nature.

vii. A member of a force or civilian component shall not be subject to any proceedings for the enforcement of any judgment given against him in the receiving State in a matter arising from the performance of his official duties.

viii. Except in so far as sub-paragraph e. of this paragraph applies to claims covered by paragraph 2 of this Article, the provisions of this paragraph shall not apply to any claim arising out of or in connexion with the navigation or operation of a ship or the loading, carriage, or discharge of a cargo, other than claims for death or personal injury to which paragraph 4 of this Article does not apply.

- Claims against members of a force or civilian component arising out of tortious acts or omissions in the receiving State not done in the performance of official duty shall be dealt with in the following manner:

i. The authorities of the receiving State shall consider the claim and assess compensation to the claimant in a fair and just manner, taking into account all the circumstances of the case, including the conduct of the injured person, and shall prepare a report on the matter.

ii. The report shall be delivered to the authorities of the sending State, who shall then decide without delay whether they will offer an *ex gratia* payment, and if so, of what amount.

iii. If an offer of *ex gratia* payment is made, and accepted by the claimant in full satisfaction of his claim, the authorities of the sending State shall make the payment themselves and inform the authorities of the receiving State of their decision and of the sum paid.

iv. Nothing in this paragraph shall affect the jurisdiction of the courts of the receiving State to entertain an action against a member of a force or of a civilian component unless and until there has been payment in full satisfaction of the claim.

- Claims arising out of the unauthorized use of any vehicle of the armed services of a sending State shall be dealt with in accordance with paragraph 6 of this Article, except in so far as the force or civilian component is legally responsible.

- If a dispute arises as to whether a tortious act or omission of a member of a force or civilian component was done in the performance of official duty or as to whether the use of any vehicle of the armed services of a sending State was unauthorized, the question shall be submitted to an arbitrator appointed in accordance with paragraph 2 b. of this Article, whose decision on this point shall be final and conclusive.

- The sending State shall not claim immunity from the jurisdiction of the courts of the receiving State for members of a force or civilian component in respect of the civil jurisdiction of the courts of the receiving State except to the extent provided in paragraph 5 g. of this Article.

- The authorities of the sending State and of the receiving State shall co-operate in the procurement of evidence for a fair hearing and disposal of claims in regard to which the Contracting Parties are concerned.

Article IX

1. Members of a force or of a civilian component and their dependents may purchase locally goods necessary for their own consumption, and such services as they need, under the same conditions as the nationals of the receiving State.

2. Goods which are required from local sources for the subsistence of a force or civilian component shall normally be purchased through the authorities which purchase such goods for the armed services of the receiving State. In order to avoid such purchases having any adverse effect on the economy of the receiving State, the competent authorities of that State shall indicate, when necessary, any articles the purchase of which should be restricted or forbidden.

3. Subject to agreements already in force or which may hereafter be made between the authorised representatives of the sending and receiving States, the authorities of the receiving State shall assume sole responsibility for making suitable arrangements to make available to a force or a civilian component the buildings and grounds which it requires, as well as facilities and services connected therewith. These agreements and arrangements shall be, as far as possible, in accordance with the regulations governing the accommodation and billeting of similar personnel of the receiving State. In the absence of a specific contract to the contrary, the laws of the receiving State shall determine the rights and obligations arising out of the occupation or use of the buildings, grounds, facilities or services.

4. Local civilian labour requirements of a force or civilian component shall be satisfied in the same way as the comparable requirements of the receiving State and with the assistance of the authorities of the receiving State through the employment exchanges. The conditions of employment and work, in particular wages, supplementary payments and conditions for the protection of workers, shall be those laid down by the legislation of the receiving State. Such civilian workers employed by a force or civilian component shall not be regarded for any purpose as being members of that force or civilian component.

5. When a force or a civilian component has at the place where it is stationed inadequate medical or dental facilities, its members and their dependents may receive medical and dental care, including hospitalization, under the same conditions as comparable personnel of the receiving State.

6. The receiving State shall give the most favourable consideration to requests for the grant to members of a force or of a civilian component of travelling facilities and concessions with regard to fares. These facilities

and concessions will be the subject of special arrangements to be made between the Governments concerned.

7. Subject to any general or particular financial arrangements between the Contracting Parties, payment in local currency for goods, accommodation and services furnished under paragraphs, 2, 3, 4 and, if necessary, 5 and 6, of this Article shall be made promptly by the authorities of the force.

8. Neither a force, nor a civilian component, nor the members thereof, nor their dependents, shall by reason of this Article enjoy any exemption from taxes or duties relating to purchases and services chargeable under the fiscal regulations of the receiving State.

Article X

1. Where the legal incidence of any form of taxation in the receiving State depends upon residence or domicile, periods during which a member of a force or civilian component is in the territory of that State by reason solely of his being a member of such force or civilian component shall not be considered as periods of residence therein, or as creating a change of residence or domicile, for the purposes of such taxation. Members of a force or civilian component shall be exempt from taxation in the receiving State on the salary and emoluments paid to them as such members by the sending State or on any tangible movable property the presence of which in the receiving State is due solely to their temporary presence there.

2. Nothing in this Article shall prevent taxation of a member of a force or civilian component with respect to any profitable enterprise, other than his employment as such member, in which he may engage in the receiving State, and, except as regards his salary and emoluments and the tangible movable property referred to in paragraph I, nothing in this Article shall prevent taxation to which, even if regarded as having his residence or domicile outside the territory of the receiving State, such a member is liable under the law of that State.

3. Nothing in this Article shall apply to 'duty' as defined in paragraph 12 of Article XI.

4. For the purposes of this Article the term 'member of a force' shall not include any person who is a national of the receiving State.

Article XI

1. Save as provided expressly to the contrary in this Agreement, members of a force and of a civilian component as well as their dependents shall be subject to the laws and regulations administered by the customs authorities of the receiving State. In particular the customs authorities of the receiving State shall have the right, under the general conditions laid

down by the laws and regulations of the receiving State, to search members of a force or civilian component and their dependents and to examine their luggage and vehicles, and to seize articles pursuant to such laws and regulations.

2.

   a. The temporary importation and the re-exportation of service vehicles of a force or civilian component under their own power shall be authorized free of duty on presentation of a triptyque in the form shown in the Appendix to this Agreement.

   b. The temporary importation of such vehicles not under their own power shall be governed by paragraph 4 of this Article and the re-exportation thereof by paragraph 8.

   c. Service vehicles of a force or civilian component shall be exempt from any tax payable in respect of the use of vehicles on the roads.

3. Official documents under official seal shall not be subject to customs inspection. Couriers, whatever their status, carrying these documents must be in possession of an individual movement order, issued in accordance with paragraph 2 b. of Article III. This movement order shall show the number of despatches carried and certify that they contain only official documents.

4. A force may import free of duty the equipment for the force and reasonable quantities of provisions, supplies and other goods for the exclusive use of the force and, in cases where such use is permitted by the receiving State, its civilian component and dependents. This duty-free importation shall be subject to the deposit, at the customs office for the place of entry, together with such customs documents as shall be agreed, of a certificate in a form agreed between the receiving State and the sending State signed by a person authorized by the sending State for that purpose. The designation of the person authorised to sign the certificates as well as specimens of the signatures and stamps to be used, shall be sent to the customs administration of the receiving State.

5. A member of a force or civilian component may, at the time of his first arrival to take up service in the receiving State or at the time of the first arrival of any dependent to join him, import his personal effects and furniture free of duty for the term of such service.

6. Members of a force or civilian component may import temporarily free of duty their private motor vehicles for the personal use of themselves and their dependents. There is no obligation under this Article to grant exemption from taxes payable in respect of the use of roads by private vehicles.

7. Imports made by the authorities of a force other than for the exclusive use of that force and its civilian component, and imports, other than those dealt with in paragraphs 5 and 6 of this Article, effected by members of a force or civilian component are not, by reason of this Article, entitled to any exemption from duty or other conditions.

8. Goods which have been imported duty-free under paragraphs 2 b., 4, 5 or 6 above:

   a. may be re-exported freely, provided that, in the case of goods imported under paragraph 4, a certificate, issued in accordance with that paragraph, is presented to the customs office: the customs authorities, however, may verify that goods re-exported are as described in the certificate, if any, and have in fact been imported under the conditions of paragraphs 2 b., 4, 5 or 6 as the case may be;

   b. shall not normally be disposed of in the receiving State by way of either sale or gift: however, in particular cases such disposal may be authorized on conditions imposed by the authorities concerned of the receiving State (for instance, on payment of duty and tax and compliance with the requirements of the controls of trade and exchange).

9. Goods purchased in the receiving State shall be exported therefrom only in accordance with the regulations in force in the receiving State.

10. Special arrangements for crossing frontiers shall be granted by the customs authorities to regularly constituted units or formations, provided that the customs authorities concerned have been duly notified in advance.

11. Special arrangements shall be made by the receiving State so that fuel, oil and lubricants for use in service vehicles, aircraft and vessels of a force or civilian component, may be delivered free of all duties and taxes.

12. In paragraphs 1-10 of this Article:
    'duty' means customs duties and all other duties and taxes payable on importation or exportation. as the case may be. except dues and taxes which are no more than charges for services rendered;
    'importation' includes withdrawal from customs warehouses or continuous customs custody, provided that the goods concerned have not been grown, produced or manufactured in the receiving State.

13. The provisions of this Article shall apply to the goods concerned not only when they are imported into or exported from the receiving State but also when they are in transit through the territory of a Contracting Party, and for this purpose the expression 'receiving State' in this Article

shall be regarded as including any Contracting Party through whose territory the goods are passing in transit.

Article XII

1. The customs or fiscal authorities of the receiving State may, as a condition of the grant of any customs or fiscal exemption or concession provided for in this Agreement, require such conditions to be observed as they may deem necessary to prevent abuse.
2. These authorities may refuse any exemption provided for by this Agreement in respect of the importation into the receiving State of articles grown, produced or manufactured in that State which have been exported therefrom without payment of, or upon repayment of, taxes or duties which would have been chargeable but for such exportation. Goods removed from a customs warehouse shall be deemed to be imported if they were regarded as having been exported by reason of being deposited in the warehouse.

Article XIII

1. In order to prevent offences against customs and fiscal laws regulations, the authorities of the receiving and of the sending States shall assist each other in the conduct of enquiries and the collection of evidence.
2. The authorities of a force shall render all assistance within their power to ensure that articles liable to seizure by, or on behalf of, the customs or fiscal authorities of the receiving State are handed to those authorities.
3. The authorities of a force shall render all assistance within their power to ensure the payment of duties, taxes and penalties payable by members of the force or civilian component or their dependents.
4. Service vehicles and articles belonging to a force or to its civilian component, and not to a member of such force or civilian component, seized by the authorities of the receiving State in connection with an offence against its customs or fiscal laws or regulations shall be handed over to the appropriate authorities of the force concerned.

Article XIV

a. A force, a civilian component and the members thereof, as well as their dependents, shall remain subject to the foreign exchange regulations of the sending State and shall also be subject to the regulations of the receiving State.
b. The foreign exchange authorities of the sending and the receiving States may issue special regulations applicable to a force or civilian component or the members thereof as well as to their dependents.

Article XV

1. Subject to paragraph 2 of this Article, this Agreement shall remain in force in the event of hostilities to which the North Atlantic Treaty applies, except that the provisions for settling claims in paragraphs 2 and 5 of Article VIII shall not apply to war damage, and that the provisions of the Agreement, and, in particular of Articles III and VII, shall immediately be reviewed by the Contracting Parties concerned, who may agree to such modifications as they may consider desirable regarding the application of the Agreement between them.

2. In the event of such hostilities, each of the Contracting Parties shall have the right, by giving 60 days' notice to the other Contracting Parties, to suspend the application of any of the provisions of this Agreement so far as it is concerned. If this right is exercised, the Contracting Parties shall immediately consult with a view to agreeing on suitable provisions to replace the provisions suspended.

Article XVI

All differences between the Contracting Parties relating to the interpretation or application of this Agreement shall be settled by negotiation between them without recourse to any outside jurisdiction. Except where express provision is made to the contrary in this Agreement, differences which cannot be settled by direct negotiation shall be referred to the North Atlantic Council.

Article XVII

Any Contracting Party may at any time request the revision of any Article of this Agreement. The request shall be addressed to the North Atlantic Council.

Article XVIII

1. The present Agreement shall be ratified and the instruments of ratification shall be deposited as soon as possible with the Government of the United States of America, which shall notify each signatory State of the date of deposit thereof.

2. Thirty days after four signatory States have deposited their instruments of ratification the present Agreement shall come into force between them. It shall come into force for each other signatory State thirty days after the deposit of its instrument of ratification.

3. After it has come into force, the present Agreement shall, subject to the approval of the North Atlantic Council and to such conditions as it may decide, be open to accession on behalf of any State which accedes to the North Atlantic Treaty. Accession shall be effected by the deposit of an

instrument of accession with the Government of the United States of America, which shall notify each signatory and acceding State of the date of deposit thereof. In respect of any State on behalf of which an instrument of accession is deposited, the present Agreement shall come into force thirty days after the date of the deposit of such instrument.

Article XIX

1. The present Agreement may be denounced by any Contracting Party after the expiration of a period of four years from the date on which the Agreement comes into force.
2. The denunciation of the Agreement by any Contracting Party shall be effected by a written notification addressed by that Contracting Party to the Government of the United States of America which shall notify all the other Contracting Parties of each such notification and the date of receipt thereof.
3. The denunciation shall take effect one year after the receipt of the notification by the Government of the United States of America. After the expiration of this period of one year, the Agreement shall cease to be in force as regards the Contracting Party which denounces it, but shall continue in force for the remaining Contracting Parties.

Article XX

1. Subject to the provisions of paragraphs 2 and 3 of this Article, the present Agreement shall apply only to the metropolitan territory of a Contracting Party.
2. Any State may, however, at the time of the deposit of its instrument of ratification or accession or at any time thereafter, declare by notification given to the Government of the United States of America that the present Agreement shall extend (subject, if the State making the declaration considers it to be necessary, to the conclusion of a special agreement between that State and each of the sending States concerned), to all or any of the territories for whose international relations it is responsible in the North Atlantic Treaty area. The present Agreement shall then extend to the territory or territories named therein thirty days after the receipt by the Government of the United States of America of the notification, or thirty days after the conclusion of the special agreements if required, or when it has come into force under Article XVIII, whichever is the later.
3. A State which has made a declaration under paragraph 2 of this Article extending the present Agreement to any territory for whose international relations it is responsible may denounce the Agreement separately in respect of that territory in accordance with the provisions of Article XIX.

In witness whereof the undersigned Plenipotentiaries have signed the present Agreement. Done in London this nineteenth day of June, 1951, in the English and French languages, both texts being equally authoritative, in a single original which shall be deposited in the archives of the Government of the United States of America. The Government of the United States of America shall transmit certified copies thereof to all the signatory and acceding States.

Protocol
On the Status of International Military Headquarters Set up Pursuant to the North Atlantic Treaty

The parties to the North Atlantic Treaty signed in Washington on 4th April, 1949,

Considering that international military Headquarters may be established in their territories, by separate arrangement, under the North Atlantic Treaty, and Desiring to define the status of such Headquarters and of the personnel thereof within the North Atlantic Treaty area,

Have agreed to the present Protocol to the Agreement signed in London on 19th June, 1951, regarding the Status of their Forces:

Article 1
In the present Protocol the expression
a. 'the Agreement' means the Agreement signed in London on 19th June, 1951, by the Parties to the North Atlantic Treaty regarding the status of their Forces;
b. 'Supreme Headquarters' means Supreme Headquarters Allied Powers in Europe, Headquarters of the Supreme Allied Commander Atlantic and any equivalent international military Headquarters set up pursuant to the North Atlantic Treaty;
c. 'Allied Headquarters' means any Supreme Headquarters and any international military Headquarters set up pursuant to the North Atlantic Treaty which is immediately subordinate to a Supreme Headquarters;
d. 'North Atlantic Council' means the Council established by Article IX of the North Atlantic Treaty or any of its subsidiary bodies authorised to act on its behalf.

Article II
Subject to the following provisions of this Protocol, the Agreement shall apply to Allied Headquarters in the territory of a Party to the present Protocol in the North Atlantic Treaty area, and to the military and civilian personnel of such

Headquarters and their dependents included in the definitions in sub-paragraphs a., b. and c. of paragraph 1 of Article III of this Protocol, when such personnel are present in any such territory in connection with their official duties or, in the case of dependents, the official duties of their spouse or parent.

Article III

1. For the purpose of applying the Agreement to an Allied Headquarters the expressions 'force', 'civilian component' and 'dependent', wherever they occur in the Agreement shall have the meanings set out below:

   a. 'force' means the personnel attached to the Allied Headquarters who belong to the land, sea or air armed services of any Party to the North Atlantic Treaty;

   b. 'civilian component' means civilian personnel who are not stateless persons, nor nationals of any State which is not a Party to the Treaty, nor nationals of, nor ordinarily resident in the receiving State, an who are (i) attached to the Allied Headquarters and in the employ of an armed service of a Party to the North Atlantic Treaty or (ii) in such categories of civilian personnel in the employ of the Allied Headquarters as the North Atlantic Council shall decide;

   c. 'dependent' means the spouse of a member of a force or civilian component, as defined in sub-paragraphs a. and b. of this paragraph, or a child of such member depending on him or her support.

2. An Allied Headquarters shall be considered to be a force for the purposes of Article II, paragraph 2 of Article V, paragraph 10 of Article VII, paragraphs 2,3,4,7 and 8 of Article IX, and Article XIII, of the Agreement.

Article IV

The rights and obligations which the Agreement gives to or imposes upon the sending State or its authorities in respect of its forces or their civilian components or dependents shall, in respect of an Allied Headquarters and its personnel and their dependents to whom the Agreement applies in accordance with Article II of the present Protocol, be vested in or attached to the appropriate Supreme Headquarters and the authorities responsible under it, except that:

a. the right which is given by Article VII of the Agreement to the military authorities of the sending State to exercise criminal and disciplinary jurisdiction shall be vested in the military authorities of the State, if any, to whose military law the person concerned is subject;

b. the obligations imposed upon the sending state or its authorities by Article II, paragraph 4 of Article III, paragraphs 5 a. and 6 a. of Article VII paragraphs 9 and 10 of Article VIII, and Article XIII, of the Agreement, shall attach both to the Allied Headquarters and to any State whose armed service, or any member or employee of whose armed service, or the dependent of such member or employee, is concerned;

c. for the purposes of paragraphs 2 a. and 5 of Article III, and Article XIV, of the Agreement the sending State shall be, in the case of members of a force and their dependents, the State to whose armed service the member belongs, or, in the case of members of a civilian component and their dependents, the State, if any, by whose armed service the member is employed;

d. the obligations imposed on the sending State by virtue of paragraphs 6 and 7 of Article VIII of the Agreement shall attach to the State to whose armed service the person belongs whose act or omission has given rise to the claim or, in the case of a member of a civilian component, to the State by whose armed service he is employed or, if there is no such State, to the Allied Headquarters of which the person concerned is a member.

Both the State, if any, to which obligations attach under this paragraph and the Allied Headquarters concerned shall have the rights of the sending State in connection with the appointment of an arbitrator under paragraph 8 of Article VIII.

Article V

Every member of an Allied Headquarters shall have a personal identity card issued by the Headquarters showing names, date and place of birth, nationality, rank or grade, number (if any), photograph and period of validity. This card must be presented on demand.

Article VI

1. The obligations to waive claims imposed on the Contracting Parties by Article VIII of the Agreement shall attach both to the Allied Headquarters and to any Party to this Protocol concerned.

2. For the purposes of paragraphs 1 and 2 of Article VIII of the Agreement,

   a. property owned by an Allied Headquarters or by a Party to this Protocol and used by an Allied Headquarters shall be deemed to be property owned by a Contracting Party and used by its armed services;

   b. damage caused by a member of a force or civilian component as defined in paragraph 1 of Article III of this Protocol or by any other employee of an Allied Headquarters shall be deemed to be damage caused by a member or employee of the armed services of a Contracting Party;

   c. the definition of the expression 'owned by a Contacting Party' in paragraph 3 of Article VIII shall apply in respect of an Allied Headquarters.

3. The claims to which paragraph 5 of Article VIII of the Agreement applies shall include claims (other than contractual claims and claims to which paragraphs 6 or 7 of that Article apply) arising out of acts or omissions of any employees of an Allied Headquarters, or out of any other act, omission or occurrence for which an Allied Headquarters, or out of any other act, omissions or occurrence for which an Allied Headquarters is legally responsible, and causing in the territory of a receiving State to third parties, other than any of the Parties to this Protocol.

Article VII
1. The exemption from taxation accorded under Article X of the Agreement to members of a force or civilian component in respect of their salaries and emoluments shall apply, as regards personnel of an Allied Headquarters within the definitions in paragraph 1 a. and b. (i) of Article 3 of this Protocol, to salaries and emoluments paid to them as such personnel by the armed service to which they belong or by which they are employed, except that this paragraph shall not exempt any such member or employee from taxation imposed by a State of which he is a national.
2. Employees of an Allied Headquarters of categories agreed by the North Atlantic Council shall be exempted from taxation on the salaries and emoluments paid to them by the Allied Headquarters in their capacity as such employees. Any Party to the present Protocol may, however, conclude an arrangement with the Allied Headquarters whereby such Party will employ and assign to the Allied Headquarters all of its nationals (except, if such Party so desires, any not ordinarily resident within its territory) who are to serve on the staff of the Allied Headquarters and pay the salaries and emoluments of such persons from its own funds, at a scale fixes by it. The salaries and emoluments so paid may be taxed by the Party concerned but shall be exempted from taxation by any other Party. If such an arrangement is entered into by any Party to the present Protocol and is subsequently modified or terminated, Parties to the present Protocol shall no longer be bound under the first sentence of this paragraph to exempt from taxation the salaries and emoluments paid to their nationals.

Article VIII
1. For the purpose of facilitating the establishment, construction, maintenance and operation of Allied Headquarters, these Headquarters shall be relieved, so far as practicable, from duties and taxes, affecting expenditures by them in the interest of common defence and for their official and exclusive benefit, and each Party to the present Protocol shall enter

into negotiations with any Allied Headquarters operating in its territory for the purpose of concluding an agreement to give effect to this provision.

2. An Allied Headquarters shall have the rights granted to a force under Article XI of the Agreement subject to the same conditions.

3. The provisions in paragraphs 5 and 6 of Article XI of the Agreement shall not apply to nationals of the receiving States, unless such nationals belong to the armed services of a Party to this Protocol other than the receiving State.

4. The expression 'duties and taxes' in this Article does not include charges for services rendered.

Article IX

Except in so far as the North Atlantic Council may decide otherwise,

a. any assets acquired from the international funds of an Allied Headquarters under its capital budget and no longer required by the Headquarters shall be disposed of under arrangements approved by the North Atlantic Council and the proceeds shall be distributed among or credited to the Parties to the North Atlantic Treaty in the proportions in which they have contributed to the capital costs of the Headquarters. The receiving State shall have the prior right to acquire any immovable property so disposed of in its territory provided that it offers terms no less favourable than those offered by any third party;

b. any land, buildings or fixed installations provided for the use of an Allied Headquarters by the receiving State without charge to the Headquarters (other than a nominal charge) and no longer required by the Headquarters shall be handed back to the receiving State, and any increase or loss in the value of the property provided by the receiving State resulting from its use by the Headquarters shall be determined by the North Atlantic Council (taking into consideration any applicable law of the receiving State) and distributed among or credited or debited to the Parties to the North Atlantic Treaty in the proportions in which they have contributed to the capital costs of the Headquarters.

Article X

Each Supreme Headquarters shall possess juridical personality; it shall have the capacity to conclude contracts and to acquire and dispose of property. The receiving State may, however, make the exercise of such capacity subject to special arrangements between it and the Supreme Headquarters or any subordinate Allied Headquarters acting on behalf of the Supreme Headquarters.

Article XI

1. Subject to the provisions of Article VIII of the Agreement, a Supreme Headquarters may engage in legal proceedings as claimant or defendant. However, the receiving State and the Supreme Headquarters or any subordinate Allied Headquarters authorized by it may agree that the receiving State shall act on behalf of the Supreme Headquarters in any legal proceedings to which that Headquarters is a party before the courts of the receiving State.

2. No measure of execution or measure directed to the seizure or attachment of its property or funds shall be taken against any Allied Headquarters, except for the purposes of paragraph 6 a. of Article VII and Article XIII of the Agreement.

Article XII

1. To enable it to operate its international budget, an Allied Headquarters may hold currency of any kind and operate accounts in any currency

2. The Parties to the present Protocol shall, at the request of an Allied Headquarters, facilitate transfers of the funds of such Headquarters from one country to another and the conversion of any currency held by an Allied Headquarters into any other currency, when necessary to meet the requirements of any Allied Headquarters.

Article XII

The archives and other official documents of an Allied Headquarters kept in premises used by those Headquarters or in the possession of any properly authorized member of the Headquarters shall be inviolable, unless the Headquarters has waived this immunity. The Headquarters shall, at the request of the receiving State and in the presence of a representative of that State, verify the nature of any documents to confirm that they are entitled to immunity under this Article.

Article XIV

1. The whole or any part of the present Protocol or of the Agreement may be applied, by decision of the North Atlantic Council, to any international military Headquarters or organization (not included in the definitions in paragraphs b. and c. of Article I of this Protocol) which is established pursuant to the North Atlantic Treaty.

2. When the European Defence Community comes into being, the present Protocol may be applied to the personnel of the European Defence Forces attached to an Allied Headquarters and their dependents at such

time and in such manner as may be determined by the North Atlantic Council

Article XV

All differences between the Parties to the present Protocol or between any such Parties and any Allied Headquarters relating to the interpretation or application of the Protocol shall be settled by negotiation between the parties in dispute without recourse to any outside jurisdiction. Except where express provision is made to the contrary in the present Protocol or in the Agreement, differences which cannot be settled by direct negotiation shall be referred to the North Atlantic Council.

Article XVI

1. Articles XV and XVII to XX of the Agreement shall apply as regards the present Protocol as if they were an integral part thereof, but so that the Protocol may be reviewed, suspended, ratified, acceded to, denounced or extended in accordance with those provisions independently from the Agreement.
2. The present Protocol may be supplemented by bilateral agreement between the receiving State and a Supreme Headquarters, and the authorities of a receiving State and a Supreme Headquarters may agree to give effect, by administrative means in advance of ratification, to any provisions of this Protocol or of the Agreement as applied by it.

In witness whereof the undersigned Plenipotentiaries have signed the present Protocol. Done in Paris this 28th day of August 1952, in the English and French languages, both texts being equally authoritative, in a single original which shall be deposited in the archives of the Government of the United States of America. The Government of the United States of America shall transmit certified copies thereof to all the signatory and acceding States.

Agreement among the States parties to the North Atlantic Treaty and the other States participating in the Partnership for Peace regarding the status of their forces

The States Parties to the North Atlantic Treaty done in Washington on 4 April 1949 and the States which accept the invitation to the Partnership for Peace issued and signed by the Heads of State and Government of the member States of the North Atlantic Treaty Organisation in Brussels on 10 January 1994 and which subscribe to the Partnership for Peace Framework Document;

Constituting together the States participating in the Partnership for Peace;

Considering that the forces of one State Party to the Present Agreement may be sent and received, by arrangement, into the territory of another State Party;

Bearing in mind that the decisions to send and to receive forces will continue to be the subject of separate arrangements between the States Parties concerned;

Desiring, however, to define the status of such forces while in the territory of another State Party;

Recalling the Agreement between the States Parties to the North Atlantic Treaty regarding the status of their forces done at London on 19 June 1951;

Have agreed as follows:

Article I:

Except as otherwise provided for in the Present Agreement and any Additional Protocol in respect to its own Parties, all States Parties to the Present Agreement shall apply the provisions of the Agreement between Parties to the North Atlantic Treaty regarding the status of their forces, done at London on 19 June 1951, hereinafter referred to as the NATO SOFA, as if all State Parties to the Present Agreement were Parties to the NATO SOFA.

Article II:
1. In addition to the area to which the NATO SOFA applies the Present Agreement shall apply to the territory of all States Parties to the Present Agreement, which are not Parties to the NATO SOFA.
2. For the purpose of the Present Agreement, references in the NATO SOFA to the North Atlantic Treaty area shall be deemed also to include the territories referred to in paragraph 1 of the present Article, and references to the North Atlantic Treaty shall be deemed to include the Partnership for Peace.

Article III:
For purposes of implementing the Present Agreement with respect to matters involving Parties that are not Parties to the NATO SOFA, provisions of the NATO SOFA that provide for requests to be submitted, or differences to be referred to the North Atlantic Council, the Chairman of the North Atlantic Council Deputies or an arbitrator shall be construed to require the Parties concerned to negotiate between or among themselves without recourse to any outside jurisdiction.

Article IV:
The Present Agreement may be supplemented or otherwise modified in accordance with international law.

Article V:
1. The Present Agreement shall be open for signature by any State that is either a contracting party to the NATO SOFA, or that accepts the invitation to Partnership for Peace and subscribed to the Partnership for Peace Framework Document.
2. The Present Agreement shall be subject to ratification, acceptance or approval. Instruments of ratification, acceptance or approval shall be deposited with the Government of the United States of America, which shall notify all signatory States of each such deposit.
3. Thirty days after three signatory States, at least one of which is a Party to the NATO SOFA and one which has accepted the invitation to the Partnership for Peace and subscribed to the Partnership for Peace Framework Document, have deposited their instruments of ratification, acceptance or approval, the Present Agreement shall enter into force in

respect of those States. It shall enter into force in respect of each other signatory State thirty days after the date of deposit of its instrument.

Article VI:

The Present Agreement may be denounced by any Party to this Agreement by giving written notification of denunciation to the Government of the United States of America, which will notify all signatory States of each such notification. The denunciation shall take effect one year after receipt of the notification by the Government of the United States of America. After the expiration of this period of one year, the Present Agreement shall cease to be in force as regards the Party that denounces it, except for the settlement of outstanding claims that arose before the day on which the denunciation takes effect, but shall continue to be in force for the remaining Parties.

In witness whereof, the undersigned, being duly authorised by their respective Governments, have signed this Agreement.

Done in Brussels, this nineteenth day of June, 1995

In the English and French languages, both texts being equally authoritative, in a single original which shall be deposited in the archives of the Government of the United States of America. The Government of the United States of America shall transmit certified copies thereof to all the signatory States.

Additional Protocol
To the Agreement among the States Parties to the North Atlantic Treaty and the other States participating in the Partnership for Peace regarding the status of their forces

The State Parties to the Present Additional Protocol to the Agreement among the State Parties to the North Atlantic Treaty and the other States participating in the Partnership for Peace regarding the status of their forces, hereinafter referred to as the Agreement;

Considering that the death penalty is not provided for under the domestic legislation of some Parties to the Agreement;

Have agreed as follows:

Article I:

Insofar as it has jurisdiction according to the provisions of the Agreement, each State Party to the Present Additional Protocol shall not carry out a death sentence with regard to any member of a force and its civilian component, and their dependents from any other State Party to the Present Additional Protocol.

Article II:

1. The Present Protocol shall be open for signature by any signatory of the Agreement.
2. The Present Protocol shall be subject to ratification, acceptance or approval. Instruments of ratification, acceptance or approval shall be deposited with the Government of the United States of America, which shall notify all signatory States of each such deposit.
3. The Present Protocol shall enter into force 30 days after the date of deposit of the instrument of ratification, acceptance or approval by three signatory States, at least one of which is a Party to the NATO SOFA and one of which is a State having accepted the invitation to join the

Partnership for Peace and having subscribed to the Partnership for Peace Framework Document.

4. The Present Protocol shall come into force in respect of each other signatory State on the date of the deposit of its instrument of ratification, acceptance or approval with the Government of the United States of America.

Done in Brussels, this nineteenth day of June, 1995

In the English and French languages, both texts being equally authoritative, in a single original which shall be deposited in the archives of the Government of the United States of America. The Government of the United States of America shall transmit certified copies thereof to all the signatory States.

Further Additional Protocol to the Agreement among the States Parties to the North Atlantic Treaty and the Other States participating in the Partnership for Peace regarding the Status of their Forces

Considering the "Agreement among the States Parties to the North Atlantic Treaty and the other States Participating in the Partnership for Peace regarding the Status of their Forces" and the Additional Protocol thereto, both done at Brussels,
June 19, 1995;

Considering the need to establish and regulate the status of NATO military headquarters and headquarters personnel in the territory of States participating in the Partnership for Peace in order to facilitate the relationship with the Armed Forces of individual Partnership for Peace nations;

Considering the need to provide appropriate status for personnel of the Armed Forces of Partner States attached to or associated with NATO military headquarters; and
Considering that the circumstances in particular NATO Member States or Partner States may make it desirable to meet the needs described above through the means of the present Protocol;

The Parties to the present Protocol have agreed as follows:

ARTICLE I
For purposes of the present Protocol, the expression
1. "Paris Protocol" means the "Protocol on the Status of International Military Headquarters set up pursuant to the North Atlantic Treaty," done at Paris, August 28, 1952.
   a. The "Agreement," wherever the expression appears in the Paris Protocol, shall be construed to mean the NATO Status of Forces Agreement as made applicable through the "Agreement among the

States Parties to the North Atlantic Treaty and the other States Participating in the Partnership for Peace regarding the Status of their Forces," done at Brussels, June 19, 1995.

b. The "force" and "civilian component", wherever those expressions appear in the Paris Protocol, have the meanings defined in Article 3 of the Paris Protocol and shall also include such persons attached to or associated with NATO military headquarters from other States Parties participating in the Partnership for Peace.

c. "Dependent", wherever the expression appears in the Paris Protocol, means the spouse of a member of a force or civilian component as defined in paragraph b. of the present Article, or a child of such member depending on him or her for support.

2. "PfP SOFA," wherever the expression appears in the present Protocol, means the "Agreement among the States Parties to the North Atlantic Treaty and the other States Participating in the Partnership for Peace regarding the Status of their Forces," done at Brussels, June 19, 1995.

3. "NATO" means the North Atlantic Treaty Organisation.

4. "NATO military headquarters" means Allied Headquarters and other international military headquarters or organisations falling within Article 1 and Article 14 of the Paris Protocol.

ARTICLE II

Without prejudice to the rights of States which are Members of NATO or participants in the Partnership for Peace but which are not Parties to the present Protocol, the Parties hereto shall apply provisions identical to those set forth in the Paris Protocol, except as modified in the present Protocol, with respect to the activities of NATO military headquarters and their military and civilian personnel carried out in the territory of a Party hereto.

ARTICLE III

1. In addition to the area to which the Paris Protocol applies, the present Protocol shall apply to the territory of all States Parties to the present Protocol, as described in Article II paragraph 1 of the PfP SOFA.

2. For purposes of the present Protocol, references in the Paris Protocol to the North Atlantic Treaty area shall be deemed to include the territories referred to in paragraph 1 of the present Article.

ARTICLE IV

For purposes of implementing the present Protocol with respect to matters involving Partner States, provisions of the Paris Protocol that provide for differences to be referred to the North Atlantic Council shall be construed to require the Parties concerned to negotiate between or among themselves without recourse to any outside jurisdiction.

ARTICLE V

1. The present Protocol shall be open for signature by any State that is a signatory of the PfP SOFA.
2. The present Protocol shall be subject to ratification, acceptance or approval. Instruments of ratification, acceptance or approval shall be deposited with the Government of the United States of America, which shall notify all signatory States of each such deposit.
3. As soon as two or more signatory States have deposited their instruments of ratification, acceptance or approval, the present Protocol shall come into force in respect of those States. It shall come into force in respect of each other signatory State on the date of the deposit of its instrument.

ARTICLE VI

The present Protocol may be denounced by any Party to this Protocol by giving written notification of denunciation to the Government of the United States of America, which will notify all signatory States of each such notification. The denunciation shall take effect one year after receipt of the notification by the Government of the United States of America. After the expiration of this period of one year, the present Protocol shall cease to be in force as regards the Party that denounces it, except for the settlement of outstanding claims that arose before the day on which the denunciation takes effect, but shall continue in force for the remaining Parties.

In witness whereof, the undersigned, being duly authorised, have signed this Protocol.

Nato Agreement For The Mutual Safeguarding Of Secrecy Of Inventions Relating To Defence And For Which Applications For Patents Have Been Made

The Governments of Belgium, Canada, Denmark, France, The Federal Republic of Germany, Greece, Italy, Luxembourg, The Netherlands, Norway, Portugal, Turkey, The United Kingdom and The United States of America,

Parties to the North Atlantic Treaty signed In Washington on 4th April, 1949;

desirous of encouraging economic collaboration between any or all of their Governments, as agreed in Article 2 of the Treaty;

mindful of the undertaking they have entered into under the terms of Article 3, to maintain and develop, by means of continuous and effective self-help, their individual and collective capacity to resist armed attack;

considering that the imposition of secrecy on an invention relating to defence in one of the North Atlantic Treaty Organization countries has generally as its corollary, when a patent has been applied for, or granted, the prohibition to apply for a patent for the same invention in other countries, including North Atlantic Treaty Organization countries ;

considering that the territorial limitation resulting from this prohibition may cause prejudice to the applicants for patents and consequently adversely affect economic collaboration between North Atlantic Treaty Organization countries,

considering that mutual assistance makes desirable reciprocal communication of inventions relating to defence and that in some cases such communication may be obstructed by this prohibition

considering that if the Government originating the prohibition is prepared to authorise the filing of an application for a patent in one or more of the other North Atlantic Treaty Organization countries, provided that the Governments of these countries also impose secrecy on the invention, the latter should not be free to refuse to impose secrecy

considering that provision has been made between the Governments of the Parties to the North Atlantic Treaty for the mutual protection and safeguarding of the classified information they may interchange;

Have agreed as follows:

ARTICLE I

The Governments Parties to this Agreement shall safeguard and cause to be safeguarded the secrecy of inventions for which applications for patents have been received under agreed procedures whenever the secrecy has been imposed on such inventions in the interests of national defence by the Government, hereinafter referred to as the "originating Government", which was the first to receive an application for a patent covering these inventions.

Provided that: this provision shall not prejudice the right of the originating Government to prohibit the filing of an application for a patent for the invention with one or more of the other Governments Parties to this Agreement.

The Governments Parties to this Agreement agree to develop such operational procedures as may be required to effectuate this Article.

ARTICLE II

The provisions of Article I shall be applied at the request either of the originating Government, or of the applicant for the pacent, provided that the latter produces evidence that secrecy has been imposed by the originating Government and that he has received authorisation from that Government to file his application for a secret patent in the country in question.

ARTICLE III

The Government called upon to safeguard the secrecy of an invention under the terms of Article I shall be entitled to demand from the applicant for the patent a waiver of any claim to compensation for loss or damage due solely to the imposition of secrecy on the invention as a condition prerequisite to the application of such safeguard.

ARTICLE IV

The secrecy measures imposed under Article I shall be removed only on the request of the originating Government. This Government shall give the other

Governments concerned six weeks' notice of its intention to remove its own measures.

The originating Government shall take into account as far as possible, having due regard to the security of the North Atlantic Treaty Organization, the representations made by other Governments within the said six weeks' period.

ARTICLE V

This Agreement shall not prevent the signatory Governments from entering into bilateral agreements for the same purpose. Existing bilateral agreements shall remain unaffected.

ARTICLE VI

The instruments of ratification or approval of this Agreement shall be deposited as soon as possible with the Government of the United Stares of America which will inform each signatory Government of the date of deposit of each instrument.

This Agreement shall enter into force 30 days after deposit by two signatory Parties of their instruments of ratification or approval. It shall enter into force for each of the other signatory Parties 30 days after the deposit of its instrument of ratification or approval.

ARTICLE VII

This Agreement may be denounced by any contracting Party by written notice of denunciation given to the Government of the Untied States of America which will inform all the other signatory Parties of such notice. Denunciation shall take effect one year after receipt of notification by the Government of the United States of America but shall not affect obligations already contracted and the rights or prerogatives previously acquired by the signatory Parties under the provisions of this Agreement.

In witness whereof the undersigned Representatives duly authorised thereto, have signed this Agreement.

Done in PARIS this 21st day of September, 1960 in the English and French languages, both texts being equally authentic, in a single copy which shall be deposited in the archives of the Government of the United States of America which will transmit a duly certified copy to the Governments of the other signatory Parties.

Agreement Between The Parties To The North Atlantic Treaty For The Security Of Information

The Parties to the North Atlantic Treaty, signed at Washington on 4th April, 1949;

Reaffirming that effective political consultation, cooperation and planning for defence in achieving the objectives of the Treaty entail the exchange of classified information among the Parties;

Considering that provisions between the Governments of the Parties to the North Atlantic Treaty for the mutual protection and safeguarding of the classified information they may interchange are necessary;

Realising that a general framework for security standards and procedures is required;

Acting on their own behalf and on behalf of the North Atlantic Treaty Organization, have agreed as follows:

ARTICLE 1

The Parties shall:

(i) protect and safeguard:
  (a) classified information (see ANNEX I), marked as such, which is originated by NATO (see ANNEX II) or which is submitted to NATO by a member state;
  (b) classified information, marked as such, of the member states submitted to another member state in support of a NATO programme, project, or contract,

(ii) maintain the security classification of information as defined under (i) above and make every effort to safeguard it accordingly;

(iii) not use classified information as defined under (i) above for purposes other than those laid down in the Notth Atlantic Treaty and the decisions and resolutions pertaining to that Treaty;

(iv) not disclose such information as defined under (i) above to non-NATO Parties without the consent of the originator.

ARTICLE 2

Pursuant to Article 1 of this Agreement, the Parties shall ensure the establishment of a National Security Authority for NATO activities which shall implement protective security measures. The Parties shall establish and implement security standards which shall ensure a common degree of protection for classified information.

ARTICLE 3

(1) The Parties shall ensure that all persons of their respective nationality who, in the conduct of their official duties, require or may have access to information classified CONFIDENTIAL and above are appropriately cleared before they take up their duties.

(2) Security clearance procedures shall be designed to determine whether an individual can, taking into account his or her loyalty and trustworthiness, have access to classified information without constituting an unacceptable risk to security.

(3) Upon request, each of the Parties shall cooperate with the other Parties in carrying out their respective security clearance procedures.

ARTICLE 4

The Secretary General shall ensure that the relevant provisions of this Agreement are applied by NATO (see ANNEX III).

ARTICLE 5

The present Agreement in no way prevents the Parties from making other Agreements relating to the exchange of classified information originated by them and not affecting the scope of the present Agreement.

ARTICLE 6

(a) This Agreement shall be open for signature by the Parties to the North Atlantic Treaty and shall be subject to ratification, acceptance or approval. The instruments of ratification, acceptance or approval shall be deposited with the Government of the United States of America;

(b) This Agreement shall enter into force thirty days after the date of deposit by two signatory States of their instruments of ratification, acceptance or approval. It shall enter into force for each other signatory

State thirty days after the deposit of its instrument of ratification, acceptance or approval.

(c) This Agreement shall with respect to the Parties for which it entered into force supersede the "Security Agreement by the Parties to the North Atlantic Treaty Organization" approved by the North Atlantic Council in Annex A (paragraph 1) to Appendix to Enclosure to D.C. 2/7, on 19th April, 1952, and subsequently incorporated in Enclosure "A" (paragraph 1) to C-M(55)15(Final), approved by the North Atlantic Council on 2nd March, 1955.

ARTICLE 7

This Agreement shall remain open for accession by any new Party to the North Atlantic Treaty, in accordance with its own constitutional procedures. Its instrument of accession shall be deposited with the government of the United States of America. It shall enter into force in respect of each acceding State thirty days after the day of the deposit of its instrument of accession.

ARTICLE 8

The Government of the United States of America shall inform the Governments of the other Parties of the deposit of each instrument of ratification, acceptance, approval or accession.

ARTICLE 9

This Agreement may be denounced by written notice of denunciation by any Party given to the depository which shall inform all the other Parties of such notice. Such denunciation shall take effect one year after receipt of notification by the depository, but shall not affect obligations already contracted and the rights or prerogatives previously acquired by the Parties under the provisions of this Agreement.

In witness whereof the undersigned, duly authorized to this effect by their respective Governments, have signed this Agreement.

Done in Brussels, this..........day of..........xxxx in a single copy in the English and French languages, each text being equally authoritative, which shall be deposited in the archives of the Government of the United States of America and of which certified copies shall be transmitted by that Government to each of the other signatories.

ANNEX I

This Annex forms an integral part of the Agreement.

NATO classified information is defined as follows:

(a) information means knowledge that can be communicated in any form;

(b) classified information means information or material determined to require protection against unauthorized disclosure which has been so designated by security classification;

(c) the word "material" includes documents and also any item of machinery or equipment or weapons either manufactured or in the process of manufacture;

(d) the word "document" means any recorded information regardless of its physical form or characteristics, including, without limitation, written or printed matter, data processing cards and tapes, maps, chars, photographs, paintings, drawings, engravings, sketches, working notes and papers, carbon copies and ink ribbons, or reproductions by an means or process, and sound, voice, magnetic or electronic or optical or video recordings in any form, and portable ADP equipment with resident computer storage media, and removable computer storage media.

ANNEX II

This Annex forms an integral part of the Agreement.

For the purposes of the present Agreement, the term "NATO" denotes the North Atlantic Treaty Organization and the bodies governed either by the Agreement on the status of the North Atlantic Treaty Organization, National Representatives and International Staff, signed in Ottawa on 20th September, 1951 or by the Protocol on the status of International Military Headquarters set up pursuant to the North Atlantic Treaty, signed in Paris on 28th August, 1952.

ANNEX III

This Annex forms an integral part of the Agreement.

Consultation takes place with military commanders in order to respect their prerogatives.

Nato Agreement On The Communication Of Technical Information For Defence Purposes

The Governments of Belgium, Canada, Denmark, France, the Federal Republic of Germany, Greece, Italy, Luxembourg, the Netherlands, Norway, Portugal, Turkey, the United Kingdom and the United States of America;

Parties to the North Atlantic Treaty signed in Washington on 4th April, 1949;

Considering that Article III of the North Atlantic Treaty provides that the Parties will maintain and develop their individual and collective capacity to resist armed attack by means of self-help and mutual assistance;

Considering that such capacity could be developed inter alia by the communication among Governments Parties and NATO Organizations of proprietary technical information to assist in defence research, development and production of military equipment and material;

Considering that rights of owners of proprietary technical information thus communicated should be recognized and protected;

Have agreed on the following provisions:

ARTICLE I

For the purpose of this Agreement:

(a) the term "for defence purposes" means for strengthening the individual or collective defence capabilities of the Parties to the North Atlantic Treaty either under national, bilateral or multilateral programmes, or in the implementation of NATO research, development, production or logistics projects;

(b) the term "proprietary technical information" means information which is technical in character, sufficiently explicit for use and has utility in industry, and which is known only to the owner and persons in privity with him and therefore not available to the public. Proprietary technical information may include, for example, inventions, drawings, know-how and data;

(c) the term "NATO Organization" means the North Atlantic Council and any subsidiary civilian or military body, including International Military Headquarters, to which apply the provisions of either the Agreement on the Status of the North Atlantic Treaty Organization, National Representatives and International Staff signed in Ottawa on 20th September, 1951, or the Protocol on the Status of International Military Headquarters set up pursuant to the North Atlantic Treaty, signed in Paris on 28th August, 1952;

(d) the term "Government or Organization of Origin" means the Government Party to this Agreement or NATO Organization first communicating technical information as being proprietary;

(e) the term "Recipient" means any Government Party to this Agreement or any NATO Organization receiving technical information communicated as proprietary either directly by the Government or Organization of Origin or through another Recipient;

(f) the term "disclosure in confidence" means disclosure of technical information to a limited number of persons who undertake not to disclose the information further except under the conditions specified by the Government or Organization of Origin;

(g) the term "unauthorized disclosure" refers to any communication of proprietary technical information which is not in accordance with the conditions under which it was communicated to the Recipient;

(h) the term "unauthorized use" refers to any use of proprietary technical information made without prior authorization or not in accordance with the conditions under which it was communicated to a Recipient.

ARTICLE II

A. When for defence purposes, technical information is communicated by a Government or Organization of Origin, to one or more Recipients as proprietary technical information, each Recipient shall, subject to the provisions of paragraph B of this Article, be responsible for safeguarding this information as proprietary technical information which has been disclosed in confidence. The Recipient shall treat this technical information in accordance with any conditions imposed and take appropriate steps compatible with these conditions to prevent this information from being communicated to anyone, published or used without authorization or treated in any other manner likely to cause damage to the owner. If a Recipient should desire to have the imposed conditions modified, this Recipient shall, unless otherwise agreed, address any request to this effect to the Government or Organization of Origin from which the proprietary technical information was received.

B. If a Recipient ascertains that any part of the technical information communicated to it as proprietary technical information was, at the time of the communication, already in its possession or available to it, or was then or at any time becomes available to the public, the Recipient shall, so far as security requirements permit, notify the Government or Organization of Origin of that fact as soon as possible and if necessary make any appropriate arrangements with the latter for continuation of confidence, for maintenance of defence security and for return of documents.

C. Nothing in this Agreement shall be considered as limiting any defence available to a Recipient in any disagreement resulting from any communication of technical information.

ARTICLE III

A. If the owner of proprietary technical information which has been communicated for defence purposes suffers damage through unauthorized disclosure or use of the information by a Recipient or anyone to whom this Recipient has disclosed the information, this Recipient shall compensate the owner:

- when it is a government, in conformity with the national law of this Recipient;

- when it is a NATO Organization, unless otherwise agreed by the parties concerned, in conformity with the law of the country in which-the Headquarters of this Organization is located.

Such compensation shall be made either directly to the owner or to the Government or Organization of Origin if the latter itself compensates the owner. In the latter case, the amount to be paid by the Recipient, will not be affected by the amount of compensation paid by the Government or Organization of Origin, unless otherwise agreed.

B. Recipients and the Government or Organization of Origin, so far as their security requirements permit, shall furnish each other with any evidence and in-formation available and accord other appropriate assistance to determine damage and compensation.

C. At the request of a Government Party to this Agreement or a NATO Organization concerned, an Advisory Committee composed solely of representatives of the Governments and NATO Organizations involved in the transaction may be created to investigate and examine evidence and report to the parties concerned on the origin, nature and scope of any damage. This Committee may request the Secretary General of the North Atlantic Treaty Organization to designate a member of the International Staff to be a member of the Committee as an observer or as a representative of the Secretary General.

D. Nothing in this Article shall impair any rights that the injured owner may have against any Government or NATO Organization.

ARTICLE IV

The Governments Parties to this Agreement shall develop within the North Atlantic Council procedures for/the implementation of this Agreement. In particular these procedures shall contain provisions governing:

(a) the communication, receipt and use of proprietary technical information under this Agreement;

(b) the participation of NATO Organizations in the communication, receipt and use of proprietary technical information;

(c) the creation and operation of the Advisory Committee provided for in Article III. C., above;

(d) requests for changes of conditions imposed on proprietary technical information, as envisaged by Article II. A, above.

ARTICLE V

1. Nothing in this Agreement shall be interpreted as affecting security commitments between or amongst Governments Parties to this Agreement.

2. Each Recipient shall accord to all proprietary technical information made available to it under the terms of this Agreement at least the same degree of security as that technical information has been accorded by the Government or Organization of Origin.

ARTICLE VI

1. Nothing in this Agreement shall prevent the Governments Parties from continuing existing agreements or entering into new agreements among themselves for this same purpose.

2. Nothing in this Agreement shall be interpreted as affecting the provisions of the NATO Agreement for the Mutual Safeguarding of Secrecy of Inventions relating to Defence and for which Applications for Patents have been made, signed in Paris on Zlst September, 1960.

ARTICLE VII

Nothing in this Agreement shall apply to the communication or use of technical information relating to atomic energy.

ARTICLE VIII

A. The instruments of ratification-or approval of this Agreement shall be deposited as soon as possible with the Government of the United States of America which will inform each signatory Government and the NATO Secretary General of the date of deposit of each instrument.

This Agreement shall enter into force 30 days after deposit by two signatory Parties of their instruments of ratification or approval. It shall enter into force for each of the other signatory Parties 30 days after the deposit of its instruments of ratification or approval.

B. The North Atlantic Council will fix the date on which the present Agreement will begin or will cease to apply to NATO Organizations.

ARTICLE IX

Any Party may cease to be a party to this Agreement one year after its notice of denunciation has been given to the Government of the United States of America, which will inform the other signatory Governments and the -Secretary General of the North Atlantic Treaty Organization of the deposit of each notice of denunciation. Denunciation shall not, however, affect obligations already contracted and the rights or prerogatives previously acquired by Parties under the provisions of this Agreement.

In witness whereof the undersigned representatives duly authorized thereto, have signed this Agreement.

Done in Brussels this 19th day of October, 1970 in the English and French languages, both texts being equally authentic, in a single copy which shall be deposited in the archives of the Government of the United States of America, which will transmit a duly certified copy to the other signatory Governments and to the Secretary General of the North Atlantic Treaty Organization.

Partnership for Peace: Invitation Document issued by the Heads of State and government participating in the Meeting of the North Atlantic Council

Brussels, 10 January 1994

We, the Heads of State and Government of the member countries of the North Atlantic Alliance, building on the close and longstanding partnership among the North American and European Allies, are committed to enhancing security and stability in the whole of Europe.

We therefore wish to strengthen ties with the democratic states to our East. We reaffirm that the Alliance, as provided for in Article 10 of the Washington Treaty, remains open to the membership of other European states in a position to further the principles of the Treaty and to contribute to the security of the North Atlantic area. We expect and would welcome NATO expansion that would reach to democratic states to our East, as part of an evolutionary process, taking into account political and security developments in the whole of Europe.

We have today launched an immediate and practical programme that will transform the relationship between NATO and participating states. This new programme goes beyond dialogue and cooperation to forge a real partnership—a Partnership for Peace. We therefore invite the other states participating in the NACC and other CSCE countries able and willing to contribute to this programme, to join with us in this partnership. Active participation in the Partnership for Peace will play an important role in the evolutionary process of the expansion of NATO.

The Partnership for Peace, which will operate under the authority of the North Atlantic Council, will forge new security relationships between the North Atlantic Alliance and its Partners for Peace. Partner states will be invited by the North Atlantic Council to participate in political and military bodies at NATO Headquarters with respect to Partnership activities.

The Partnership will expand and intensify political and military cooperation throughout Europe, increase stability, diminish threats to peace, and build strengthened relationships by promoting the spirit of practical cooperation and commitment to democratic principles that underpin our Alliance. NATO will consult with any active participant in the Partnership if that partner perceives a direct threat to its territorial integrity, political independence, or security. At a pace and scope determined by the capacity and desire of the individual participating states, we will work in concrete ways towards transparency in defence budgeting, promoting democratic control of defence ministries, joint planning, joint military exercises, and creating an ability to operate with NATO forces in such fields as peacekeeping, search and rescue and humanitarian operations, and others as may be agreed.

To promote closer military cooperation and interoperability, we will propose, within the Partnership framework, peacekeeping field exercises beginning in 1994. To coordinate joint military activities within the Partnership, we will invite states participating in the Partnership to send permanent liaison officers to NATO Headquarters and a separate Partnership Coordination Cell at Mons (Belgium) that would, under the authority of the North Atlantic Council, carry out the military planning necessary to implement the Partnership programmes.

Since its inception two years ago, the North Atlantic Cooperation Council has greatly expanded the depth and scope of its activities. We will continue to work with all our NACC partners to build cooperative relationships across the entire spectrum of the Alliance's activities. With the expansion of NACC activities and the establishment of the Partnership for Peace, we have decided to offer permanent facilities at NATO Headquarters for personnel from NACC countries and other Partnership for Peace participants in order to improve our working relationships and facilitate closer cooperation.

Partnership for Peace: Framework Document issued by the Heads of State and Government participating in the Meeting of the North Atlantic Council

Brussels, 10 January 1994

1. Further to the invitation extended by the NATO Heads of State and Government at their meeting on 10/11 January, 1994, the member states of the North Atlantic Alliance and the other states subscribing to this document, resolved to deepen their political and military ties and to contribute further to the strengthening of security within the Euro-Atlantic area, hereby establish, within the framework of the North Atlantic Cooperation Council, this Partnership for Peace.

2. This Partnership is established as an expression of a joint conviction that stability and security in the Euro-Atlantic area can be achieved only through cooperation and common action. Protection and promotion of fundamental freedoms and human rights, and safeguarding of freedom, justice, and peace through democracy are shared values fundamental to the Partnership.

   In joining the Partnership, the member States of the North Atlantic Alliance and the other States subscribing to this Document recall that they are committed to the preservation of democratic societies, their freedom from coercion and intimidation, and the maintenance of the principles of international law.

   They reaffirm their commitment to fulfil in good faith the obligations of the Charter of the United Nations and the principles of the Universal Declaration on Human Rights; specifically, to refrain from the threat or use of force against the territorial integrity or political independence of any State, to respect existing borders and to settle disputes by peaceful means.

   They also reaffirm their commitment to the Helsinki Final Act and all subsequent CSCE documents and to the fulfilment of the commitments and obligations they have undertaken in the field of disarmament and arms control.

3. The other states subscribing to this document will cooperate with the North Atlantic Treaty Organisation in pursuing the following objectives:
   a. facilitation of transparency in national defence planning and budgeting processes;

b. ensuring democratic control of defence forces;
c. maintenance of the capability and readiness to contribute, subject to constitutional considerations, to operations under the authority of the UN and/or the responsibility of the CSCE;
d. the development of cooperative military relations with NATO, for the purpose of joint planning, training, and exercises in order to strengthen their ability to undertake missions in the fields of peacekeeping, search and rescue, humanitarian operations, and others as may subsequently be agreed; e. the development, over the longer term, of forces that are better able to operate with those of the members of the North Atlantic Alliance.

4. The other subscribing states will provide to the NATO Authorities Presentation Documents identifying the steps they will take to achieve the political goals of the Partnership and the military and other assets that might be used for Partnership activities. NATO will propose a programme of partnership exercises and other activities consistent with the Partnership's objectives. Based on this programme and its Presentation Document, each subscribing state will develop with NATO an individual Partnership Programme.

5. In preparing and implementing their individual Partnership Programmes, other subscribing states may, at their own expense and in agreement with the Alliance and, as necessary, relevant Belgian authorities, establish their own liaison office with NATO Headquarters in Brussels. This will facilitate their participation in NACC/Partnership meetings and activities, as well as certain others by invitation. They will also make available personnel, assets, facilities and capabilities necessary and appropriate for carrying out the agreed Partnership Programme. NATO will assist them, as appropriate, in formulating and executing their individual Partnership Programmes.

6. The other subscribing states accept the following understandings:
a. those who envisage participation in missions referred to in paragraph 3(d) will, where appropriate, take part in related NATO exercises;
b. they will fund their own participation in Partnership activities, and will endeavour otherwise to share the burdens of mounting exercises in which they take part;
c. they may send, after appropriate agreement, permanent liaison officers to a separate Partnership Coordination Cell at Mons (Belgium) that would, under the authority of the North Atlantic Council, carry out the military planning necessary to implement the Partnership programmes;
d. those participating in planning and military exercises will have access to certain NATO technical data relevant to interoperability;

e. building upon the CSCE measures on defence planning, the other sub-scribing states and NATO countries will exchange information on the steps that have been taken or are being taken to promote transparency in defence planning and budgeting and to ensure the democratic control of armed forces;

f. they may participate in a reciprocal exchange of information on defence planning and budgeting which will be developed within the framework of the NACC/Partnership for Peace.

7. In keeping with their commitment to the objectives of this Partnership for Peace, the members of the North Atlantic Alliance will:

- develop with the other subscribing states a planning and review process to provide a basis for identifying and evaluating forces and capabilities that might be made available by them for multinational training, exercises, and operations in conjunction with Alliance forces;

- promote military and political coordination at NATO Headquarters in order to provide direction and guidance relevant to Partnership activities with the other subscribing states, including planning, training, exercises and the development of doctrine.

8. NATO will consult with any active participant in the Partnership if that Partner perceives a direct threat to its territorial integrity, political independence, or security.

Basic Document of the Euro-Atlantic Partnership Council

Sintra, Portugal, 30 May 1997

1. The member countries of the North Atlantic Cooperation Council and participating countries of the Partnership for Peace, determined to raise to a qualitatively new level their political and military cooperation, building upon the success of NACC and PfP, have decided to establish a Euro-Atlantic Partnership Council. In doing so, they reaffirm their joint commitment to strengthen and extend peace and stability in the Euro-Atlantic area, on the basis of the shared values and principles which underlie their cooperation, notably those set out in the Framework Document of the Partnership for Peace.

2. The Euro-Atlantic Partnership Council will be a new cooperative mechanism which will form a framework for enhanced efforts in both an expanded political dimension of partnership and practical cooperation under PfP. It will take full account of and complement the respective activities of the OSCE and other relevant institutions such as the European Union, the Western European Union and the Council of Europe.

3. The Euro-Atlantic Partnership Council, as the successor to NACC, will provide the overarching framework for consultations among its members on a broad range of political and security-related issues, as part of a process that will develop through practice. PfP in its enhanced form will be a clearly identifiable element within this flexible framework. Its basic elements will remain valid. The Euro-Atlantic Partnership Council will build upon the existing framework of NATO's outreach activities preserving their advantages to promote cooperation in a transparent way. The expanded political dimension of consultation and cooperation which the Council will offer will allow Partners, if they wish, to develop a direct political relationship individually or in smaller groups with the Alliance. In addition, the Council will provide the framework to afford Partner countries, to the maximum extent possible, increased decision-making opportunities relating to activities in which they participate.

4. The Euro-Atlantic Partnership Council will retain two important principles which have underpinned the success of cooperation between Allies and Partners so far. It will be inclusive, in that opportunities for political consultation and practical cooperation will be open to all Allies and Partners equally. It will also maintain self-differentiation, in that Partners will be able to decide for themselves

the level and areas of cooperation with NATO. Arrangements under the Council will not affect commitments already undertaken bilaterally between Partners and NATO, or commitments in the PfP Framework Document including the consultation provisions of its article 8.

5. The Euro-Atlantic Partnership Council will meet, as required, in different formats:

In plenary session to address political and security-related issues of common concern and to provide information as appropriate on activities with limited participation.

In a limited format between the Alliance and open-ended groups of Partners to focus on functional matters or, on an ad hoc basis, on appropriate regional matters. In such cases, the other EAPC members will be kept informed about the results.

In a limited format between the Alliance and groups of Partners who participate with NATO in a peace support operation or in the Planning and Review Process, or in other cases for which this format has been agreed. The other members of the EAPC will be informed as appropriate.

In an individual format between the Alliance and one Partner.

STRUCTURE

6. The Euro-Atlantic Partnership Council will meet, as a general rule, at Ambassadorial level in Brussels and on a monthly basis.

7. The Council will meet twice a year at both Foreign Ministers and Defence Ministers level; additional meetings can be envisaged as required. It may also meet at the level of Heads of State or Government, when appropriate.

8. The Council will be chaired by the Secretary General of the North Atlantic Alliance or his Deputy. The representative of a member country will be named President d'Honneur for six months according to modalities to be determined.

9. The work of the Euro-Atlantic Partnership Council will be supported regularly by the Political-Military Steering Committee (PMSC) and the Political Committee (PC) in their configurations at Alliance with all Partners. On an ad hoc basis an EAPC Senior Political Committee would address issues referred to it, as required. The EAPC will consider, based on evolving practical experience, whether this support could be improved by an EAPC Steering Committee (EAPC-SC) which would integrate the functions of the former enlarged Political Committee and the PMSC in NACC/PfP format.

The PMSC will meet, as appropriate, in an Alliance with individual Partners or Alliance with groups of Partners (e.g. PARP) configuration. The PMSC and PC with Partners will meet at least once a month, or more frequently if required. Other NATO Committees will expand opportunities for work with Partners on cooperation issues and will inform the EAPC on their work in this regard. Their activities will become part of the Euro-Atlantic Partnership Council framework. An important part of this framework will be new opportunities for Partner consultations with the Military Committee. The Military Committee will also play a major role in the expanded range of opportunities for consultation and cooperation provided by the future support structure for the EAPC.

SUBSTANCE

10. The Euro-Atlantic Partnership Council will adopt at the time of its establishment the NACC Work Plan for Dialogue, Partnership and Cooperation and will replace it with an EAPC Work Plan as part of its future work. The activities included in the Partnership Work Programme (PWP) will also come under the general purview of the EAPC.

11. Specific subject areas on which Allies and Partners would consult, in the framework of the EAPC, might include but not be limited to: political and security related matters; crisis management; regional matters; arms control issues; nuclear, biological and chemical (NBC) proliferation and defence issues; international terrorism; defence planning and budgets and defence policy and strategy; security impacts of economic developments. There will also be scope for consultations and cooperation on issues such as: civil emergency and disaster preparedness; armaments cooperation under the aegis of the Conference of National Armaments Directors (CNAD); nuclear safety; defence related environmental issues; civil-military coordination of air traffic management and control; scientific cooperation; and issues related to peace support operations.

ELIGIBILITY

12. Present NACC members and PfP participating countries automatically become members of the Euro-Atlantic Partnership Council if they so desire. The Euro-Atlantic Partnership Council is open to the accession of other OSCE participating states able and willing to accept its basic principles and to contribute to its goals. New members may join the EAPC by joining the Partnership for Peace through signing the PfP Framework Document and by stating their acceptance of the concept of the EAPC as laid out in this document. The EAPC would be invited to endorse the accession of its new members.

Founding Act on Mutual Relations, Cooperation and Security between NATO and the Russian Federation

Paris, 27 May 1997

The North Atlantic Treaty Organization and its member States, on the one hand, and the Russian Federation, on the other hand, hereinafter referred to as NATO and Russia, based on an enduring political commitment undertaken at the highest political level, will build together a lasting and inclusive peace in the Euro-Atlantic area on the principles of democracy and cooperative security.

NATO and Russia do not consider each other as adversaries. They share the goal of overcoming the vestiges of earlier confrontation and competition and of strengthening mutual trust and cooperation. The present Act reaffirms the determination of NATO and Russia to give concrete substance to their shared commitment to build a stable, peaceful and undivided Europe, whole and free, to the benefit of all its peoples. Making this commitment at the highest political level marks the beginning of a fundamentally new relationship between NATO and Russia. They intend to develop, on the basis of common interest, reciprocity and transparency a strong, stable and enduring partnership.

This Act defines the goals and mechanism of consultation, cooperation, joint decision-making and joint action that will constitute the core of the mutual relations between NATO and Russia.

NATO has undertaken a historic transformation—a process that will continue. In 1991 the Alliance revised its strategic doctrine to take account of the new security environment in Europe. Accordingly, NATO has radically reduced and continues the adaptation of its conventional and nuclear forces. While preserving the capability to meet the commitments undertaken in the Washington Treaty, NATO has expanded and will continue to expand its political functions, and taken on new missions of peacekeeping and crisis management in support of the United Nations (UN) and the Organisation for Security and Cooperation in Europe (OSCE), such as in Bosnia and Herzegovina, to address new security challenges in close association with other countries and international organisations. NATO is in the process of developing the European Security and Defence Identity (ESDI) within the Alliance. It will continue to develop a broad and dynamic pattern of cooperation with OSCE participating States in particular through the Partnership for Peace and is working with Partner countries on the initiative to establish a Euro-Atlantic Partnership Council. NATO member States have decided to examine NATO's Strategic Concept to ensure that it is fully consistent with Europe's new security situation and challenges.

Russia is continuing the building of a democratic society and the realisation of its political and economic transformation. It is developing the concept of its national security and revising its military doctrine to ensure that they are fully consistent with new security realities. Russia has carried out deep reductions in its armed forces, has withdrawn its forces on an unprecedented scale from the countries of Central and Eastern Europe and the Baltic countries and withdrawn all its nuclear weapons back to its own national territory. Russia is committed to further reducing its conventional and nuclear forces. It is actively participating in peace-keeping operations in support of the UN and the OSCE, as well as in crisis management in different areas of the world. Russia is contributing to the multinational forces in Bosnia and Herzegovina.

I. Principles

Proceeding from the principle that the security of all states in the Euro-Atlantic community is indivisible, NATO and Russia will work together to contribute to the establishment in Europe of common and comprehensive security based on the allegiance to shared values, commitments and norms of behaviour in the interests of all states.

NATO and Russia will help to strengthen the Organisation for Security and Cooperation in Europe, including developing further its role as a primary instrument in preventive diplomacy, conflict prevention, crisis management, post-conflict rehabilitation and regional security cooperation, as well as in enhancing its operational capabilities to carry out these tasks. The OSCE, as the only pan-European security organisation, has a key role in European peace and stability. In strengthening the OSCE, NATO and Russia will cooperate to prevent any possibility of returning to a Europe of division and confrontation, or the isolation of any state.

Consistent with the OSCE's work on a Common and Comprehensive Security Model for Europe for the Twenty-First Century, and taking into account the decisions of the Lisbon Summit concerning a Charter on European security, NATO and Russia will seek the widest possible cooperation among participating States of the OSCE with the aim of creating in Europe a common space of security and stability, without dividing lines or spheres of influence limiting the sovereignty of any state.

NATO and Russia start from the premise that the shared objective of strengthening security and stability in the Euro-Atlantic area for the benefit of all countries requires a response to new risks and challenges, such as aggressive nationalism, proliferation of nuclear, biological and chemical weapons, terrorism, persistent abuse of human rights and of the rights of persons belonging to national minorities and unresolved territorial disputes, which pose a threat to common peace, prosperity and stability.

This Act does not affect, and cannot be regarded as affecting, the primary responsibility of the UN Security Council for maintaining international peace and security, or the role of the OSCE as the inclusive and comprehensive organisation for consultation, decision-making and cooperation in its area and as a regional arrangement under Chapter VIII of the United Nations Charter.

In implementing the provisions in this Act, NATO and Russia will observe in good faith their obligations under international law and international instruments, including the obligations of the United Nations Charter and the provisions of the Universal Declaration on Human Rights as well as their commitments under the Helsinki Final Act and subsequent OSCE documents, including the Charter of Paris and the documents adopted at the Lisbon OSCE Summit.

To achieve the aims of this Act, NATO and Russia will base their relations on a shared commitment to the following principles:

- development, on the basis of transparency, of a strong, stable, enduring and equal partnership and of cooperation to strengthen security and stability in the Euro-Atlantic area;
- acknowledgement of the vital role that democracy, political pluralism, the rule of law, and respect for human rights and civil liberties and the development of free market economies play in the development of common prosperity and comprehensive security;
- refraining from the threat or use of force against each other as well as against any other state, its sovereignty, territorial integrity or political independence in any manner inconsistent with the United Nations Charter and with the Declaration of Principles Guiding Relations Between Participating States contained in the Helsinki Final Act;
- respect for sovereignty, independence and territorial integrity of all states and their inherent right to choose the means to ensure their own security, the inviolability of borders and peoples' right of self-determination as enshrined in the Helsinki Final Act and other OSCE documents;
- mutual transparency in creating and implementing defence policy and military doctrines;

- prevention of conflicts and settlement of disputes by peaceful means in accordance with UN and OSCE principles;
- support, on a case-by-case basis, of peacekeeping operations carried out under the authority of the UN Security Council or the responsibility of the OSCE.

II. Mechanism for Consultation and Cooperation, the NATO-Russia Permanent Joint Council

To carry out the activities and aims provided for by this Act and to develop common approaches to European security and to political problems, NATO and Russia will create the NATO-Russia Permanent Joint Council. The central objective of this Permanent Joint Council will be to build increasing levels of trust, unity of purpose and habits of consultation and cooperation between NATO and Russia, in order to enhance each other's security and that of all nations in the Euro-Atlantic area and diminish the security of none. If disagreements arise, NATO and Russia will endeavour to settle them on the basis of goodwill and mutual respect within the framework of political consultations.

The Permanent Joint Council will provide a mechanism for consultations, coordination and, to the maximum extent possible, where appropriate, for joint decisions and joint action with respect to security issues of common concern. The consultations will not extend to internal matters of either NATO, NATO member States or Russia.

The shared objective of NATO and Russia is to identify and pursue as many opportunities for joint action as possible. As the relationship develops, they expect that additional opportunities for joint action will emerge.

The Permanent Joint Council will be the principal venue of consultation between NATO and Russia in times of crisis or for any other situation affecting peace and stability. Extraordinary meetings of the Council will take place in addition to its regular meetings to allow for prompt consultations in case of emergencies. In this context, NATO and Russia will promptly consult within the Permanent Joint Council in case one of the Council members perceives a threat to its territorial integrity, political independence or security.

The activities of the Permanent Joint Council will be built upon the principles of reciprocity and transparency. In the course of their consultations and cooperation, NATO and Russia will inform each other regarding the respective security-related challenges they face and the measures that each intends to take to address them.

Provisions of this Act do not provide NATO or Russia, in any way, with a right of veto over the actions of the other nor do they infringe upon or restrict the rights of NATO or Russia to independent decision-making and action. They cannot be used as a means to disadvantage the interests of other states.

The Permanent Joint Council will meet at various levels and in different forms, according to the subject matter and the wishes of NATO and Russia. The Permanent Joint Council will meet at the level of Foreign Ministers and at the level of Defence Ministers twice annually, and also monthly at the level of ambassadors/permanent representatives to the North Atlantic Council.

The Permanent Joint Council may also meet, as appropriate, at the level of Heads of State and Government.

The Permanent Joint Council may establish committees or working groups for individual subjects or areas of cooperation on an ad hoc or permanent basis, as appropriate.

Under the auspices of the Permanent Joint Council, military representatives and Chiefs of Staff will also meet; meetings of Chiefs of Staff will take place no less than twice a year, and also monthly at military representatives level. Meetings of military experts may be convened, as appropriate.

The Permanent Joint Council will be chaired jointly by the Secretary General of NATO, a representative of one of the NATO member States on a rotation basis, and a representative of Russia.

To support the work of the Permanent Joint Council, NATO and Russia will establish the necessary administrative structures.

Russia will establish a Mission to NATO headed by a representative at the rank of Ambassador. A senior military representative and his staff will be part of this Mission for the purposes of the military cooperation. NATO retains the possibility of establishing an appropriate presence in Moscow, the modalities of which remain to be determined.

The agenda for regular sessions will be established jointly. Organisational arrangements and rules of procedure for the Permanent Joint Council will be worked out. These arrangements will be in place for the inaugural meeting of the Permanent Joint Council which will be held no later than four months after the signature of this Act.

The Permanent Joint Council will engage in three distinct activities:

- consulting on the topics in Section III of this Act and on any other political or security issue determined by mutual consent;
- on the basis of these consultations, developing joint initiatives on which NATO and Russia would agree to speak or act in parallel;
- once consensus has been reached in the course of consultation, making joint decisions and taking joint action on a case-by-case basis, including participation, on an equitable basis, in the planning and preparation of

joint operations, including peacekeeping operations under the authority of the UN Security Council or the responsibility of the OSCE.

Any actions undertaken by NATO or Russia, together or separately, must be consistent with the United Nations Charter and the OSCE's governing principles.

Recognizing the importance of deepening contacts between the legislative bodies of the participating States to this Act, NATO and Russia will also encourage expanded dialogue and cooperation between the North Atlantic Assembly and the Federal Assembly of the Russian Federation.

III. Areas for Consultation and Cooperation

In building their relationship, NATO and Russia will focus on specific areas of mutual interest. They will consult and strive to cooperate to the broadest possible degree in the following areas:

- issues of common interest related to security and stability in the Euro-Atlantic area or to concrete crises, including the contribution of NATO and Russia to security and stability in this area;
- conflict prevention, including preventive diplomacy, crisis management and conflict resolution taking into account the role and responsibility of the UN and the OSCE and the work of these organisations in these fields;
- joint operations, including peacekeeping operations, on a case-by-case basis, under the authority of the UN Security Council or the responsibility of the OSCE, and if Combined Joint Task Forces (CJTF) are used in such cases, participation in them at an early stage;
- participation of Russia in the Euro-Atlantic Partnership Council and the Partnership for Peace;
- exchange of information and consultation on strategy, defence policy, the military doctrines of NATO and Russia, and budgets and infrastructure development programmes;
- arms control issues;
- nuclear safety issues, across their full spectrum;
- preventing the proliferation of nuclear, biological and chemical weapons, and their delivery means, combatting nuclear trafficking and strengthening cooperation in specific arms control areas, including political and defence aspects of proliferation;
- possible cooperation in Theatre Missile Defence;
- enhanced regional air traffic safety, increased air traffic capacity and reciprocal exchanges, as appropriate, to promote confidence through increased measures of transparency and exchanges of information in relation to air defence and related aspects of airspace management/control.

This will include exploring possible cooperation on appropriate air defence related matters;

- increasing transparency, predictability and mutual confidence regarding the size and roles of the conventional forces of member States of NATO and Russia;
- reciprocal exchanges, as appropriate, on nuclear weapons issues, including doctrines and strategy of NATO and Russia;
- coordinating a programme of expanded cooperation between respective military establishments, as further detailed below;
- pursuing possible armaments-related cooperation through association of Russia with NATO's Conference of National Armaments Directors;
- conversion of defence industries;
- developing mutually agreed cooperative projects in defence-related economic, environmental and scientific fields;
- conducting joint initiatives and exercises in civil emergency preparedness and disaster relief;
- combatting terrorism and drug trafficking;
- improving public understanding of evolving relations between NATO and Russia, including the establishment of a NATO documentation centre or information office in Moscow.

Other areas can be added by mutual agreement.

IV. POLITICAL-MILITARY MATTERS

NATO and Russia affirm their shared desire to achieve greater stability and security in the Euro-Atlantic area.

The member States of NATO reiterate that they have no intention, no plan and no reason to deploy nuclear weapons on the territory of new members, nor any need to change any aspect of NATO's nuclear posture or nuclear policy—and do not foresee any future need to do so. This subsumes the fact that NATO has decided that it has no intention, no plan, and no reason to establish nuclear weapon storage sites on the territory of those members, whether through the construction of new nuclear storage facilities or the adaptation of old nuclear storage facilities. Nuclear storage sites are understood to be facilities specifically designed for the stationing of nuclear weapons, and include all types of hardened above or below ground facilities (storage bunkers or vaults) designed for storing nuclear weapons.

Recognising the importance of the adaptation of the Treaty on Conventional Armed Forces in Europe (CFE) for the broader context of security in the OSCE area and the work on a Common and Comprehensive Security Model for Europe for the Twenty-First Century, the member States of NATO and Russia will work together in Vienna with the other States Parties to adapt the CFE Treaty to enhance its viability and effectiveness, taking into account Europe's changing security environment and the legitimate security interests of all OSCE participating States. They share the objective of concluding an adaptation agreement as expeditiously as possible and, as a first step in this process, they will, together with other States Parties to the CFE Treaty, seek to conclude as soon as possible a framework agreement setting forth the basic elements of an adapted CFE Treaty, consistent with the objectives and principles of the Document on Scope and Parameters agreed at Lisbon in December 1996.

NATO and Russia believe that an important goal of CFE Treaty adaptation should be a significant lowering in the total amount of Treaty-Limited Equipment permitted in the Treaty's area of application compatible with the legitimate defence requirements of each State Party. NATO and Russia encourage all States Parties to the CFE Treaty to consider reductions in their CFE equipment entitlements, as part of an overall effort to achieve lower equipment levels that are consistent with the transformation of Europe's security environment.

The member States of NATO and Russia commit themselves to exercise restraint during the period of negotiations, as foreseen in the Document on Scope and Parameters, in relation to the current postures and capabilities of their conventional armed forces—in particular with respect to their levels of forces and deployments—in the Treaty's area of application, in order to avoid developments in the security situation in Europe diminishing the security of any State Party. This commitment is without prejudice to possible voluntary decisions by the individual States Parties to reduce their force levels or deployments, or to their legitimate security interests.

The member States of NATO and Russia proceed on the basis that adaptation of the CFE Treaty should help to ensure equal security for all States Parties irrespective of their membership of a politico-military alliance, both to preserve and strengthen stability and continue to prevent any destabilizing increase of forces in various regions of Europe and in Europe as a whole. An adapted CFE Treaty should also further enhance military transparency by extended information exchange and verification, and permit the possible accession by new States Parties.

The member States of NATO and Russia propose to other CFE States Parties to carry out such adaptation of the CFE Treaty so as to enable States Parties to reach, through a transparent and cooperative process, conclusions regarding reductions they might be prepared to take and resulting national Treaty-Limited Equipment ceilings. These will then be codified as binding limits in the adapted Treaty to be agreed by consensus of all States Parties, and reviewed in 2001 and at five-year intervals thereafter. In doing so, the States Parties will take into account all the levels of Treaty-Limited Equipment established for the Atlantic-to-the-Urals area by the original CFE Treaty, the substantial reductions that have been carried out since then, the changes to the situation in Europe and the need to ensure that the security of no state is diminished.

The member States of NATO and Russia reaffirm that States Parties to the CFE Treaty should maintain only such military capabilities, individually or in conjunction with others, as are commensurate with individual or collective legitimate security needs, taking into account their international obligations, including the CFE Treaty.

Each State-Party will base its agreement to the provisions of the adapted Treaty on all national ceilings of the States Parties, on its projections of the current and future security situation in Europe.

In addition, in the negotiations on the adaptation of the CFE Treaty, the member States of NATO and Russia will, together with other States Parties, seek to strengthen stability by further developing measures to prevent any potentially threatening build-up of conventional forces in agreed regions of Europe, to include Central and Eastern Europe.

NATO and Russia have clarified their intentions with regard to their conventional force postures in Europe's new security environment and are prepared to consult on the evolution of these postures in the framework of the Permanent Joint Council.

NATO reiterates that in the current and foreseeable security environment, the Alliance will carry out its collective defence and other missions by ensuring the necessary interoperability, integration, and capability for reinforcement rather than by additional permanent stationing of substantial combat forces. Accordingly, it will have to rely on adequate infrastructure commensurate with the above tasks. In this context, reinforcement may take place, when necessary, in the event of defence against a threat of aggression and missions in support of peace consistent with the United Nations Charter and the OSCE governing principles, as well as for exercises consistent with the adapted CFE Treaty, the provisions of the Vienna Document 1994 and mutually agreed transparency measures. Russia will exercise similar restraint in its conventional force deployments in Europe.

The member States of NATO and Russia will strive for greater transparency, predictability and mutual confidence with regard to their armed forces. They will comply fully with their obligations under the Vienna Document 1994 and develop cooperation with the other OSCE participating States, including negotiations in the appropriate format, inter alia within the OSCE to promote confidence and security.

The member States of NATO and Russia will use and improve existing arms control regimes and confidence-building measures to create security relations based on peaceful cooperation.

NATO and Russia, in order to develop cooperation between their military establishments, will expand political-military consultations and cooperation through the Permanent Joint Council with an enhanced dialogue between the senior military authorities of NATO and its member States and of Russia. They will implement a programme of significantly expanded military activities and practical cooperation between NATO and Russia at all levels. Consistent with the tenets of the Permanent Joint Council, this enhanced military-to-military dialogue will be built upon the principle that neither party views the other as a threat nor seeks to disadvantage the other's security. This enhanced military-to-military dialogue will include regularly-scheduled reciprocal briefings on NATO and Russian military doctrine, strategy and resultant force posture and will include the broad possibilities for joint exercises and training.

To support this enhanced dialogue and the military components of the Permanent Joint Council, NATO and Russia will establish military liaison missions at various levels on the basis of reciprocity and further mutual arrangements.

To enhance their partnership and ensure this partnership is grounded to the greatest extent possible in practical activities and direct cooperation, NATO's and Russia's respective military authorities will explore the further development of a concept for joint NATO-Russia peacekeeping operations. This initiative should build upon the positive experience of working together in Bosnia and Herzegovina, and the lessons learned there will be used in the establishment of Combined Joint Task Forces.

The present Act takes effect upon the date of its signature.

NATO and Russia will take the proper steps to ensure its implementation in accordance with their procedures.

The present Act is established in two originals in the French, English and Russian language.

The Secretary General of NATO and the Government of the Russian Federation will provide the Secretary General of the United Nations and the Secretary General of the OSCE with the text of this Act with the request to circulate it to all members of their Organisations.

Charter on a Distinctive Partnership between the North Atlantic Treaty Organization and Ukraine

Madrid, 9 July 1997

I. Building an Enhanced NATO-Ukraine Relationship

1. The North Atlantic Treaty Organization (NATO) and its member States and Ukraine, hereinafter referred to as NATO and Ukraine,

   • building on a political commitment at the highest level;

   • recognizing the fundamental changes in the security environment in Europe which have inseparably linked the security of every state to that of all the others;

   • determined to strengthen mutual trust and cooperation in order to enhance security and stability, and to cooperate in building a stable, peaceful and undivided Europe;

   • stressing the profound transformation undertaken by NATO since the end of the Cold War and its continued adaptation to meet the changing circumstances of Euro-Atlantic security, including its support, on a case-by-case basis, of new missions of peacekeeping operations carried out under the authority of the United Nations Security Council or the responsibility of the OSCE;

   • welcoming the progress achieved by Ukraine and looking forward to further steps to develop its democratic institutions, to implement radical economic reforms, and to deepen the process of integration with the full range of European and Euro-Atlantic structures;

   • noting NATO's positive role in maintaining peace and stability in Europe and in promoting greater confidence and transparency in the Euro-Atlantic area, and its openness for cooperation with the new democracies of Central and Eastern Europe, an inseparable part of which is Ukraine;

   • convinced that an independent, democratic and stable Ukraine is one of the key factors for ensuring stability in Central and Eastern Europe, and the continent as a whole;

   • mindful of the importance of a strong and enduring relationship between NATO and Ukraine and recognizing the solid progress made, across a broad range of activities, to develop an enhanced and strengthened relationship between NATO and Ukraine on the foundations created by the Joint Press Statement of 14 September 1995;

- determined to further expand and intensify their cooperation in the framework of the Euro-Atlantic Partnership Council, including the enhanced Partnership for Peace programme;
- welcoming their practical cooperation within IFOR/SFOR and other peacekeeping operations on the territory of the former Yugoslavia;
- sharing the view that the opening of the Alliance to new members, in accordance with Article 10 of the Washington Treaty, is directed at enhancing the stability of Europe, and the security of all countries in Europe without recreating dividing lines;

are committed, on the basis of this Charter, to further broaden and strengthen their cooperation and to develop a distinctive and effective partnership, which will promote further stability and common democratic values in Central and Eastern Europe.

II. Principles for the Development of NATO-Ukraine Relations

2. NATO and Ukraine will base their relationship on the principles, obligations and commitments under international law and international instruments, including the United Nations Charter, the Helsinki Final Act and subsequent OSCE documents. Accordingly, NATO and Ukraine reaffirm their commitment to:

- the recognition that security of all states in the OSCE area is indivisible, that no state should pursue its security at the expense of that of another state, and that no state can regard any part of the OSCE region as its sphere of influence;
- refrain from the threat or use of force against any state in any manner inconsistent with the United Nations Charter or Helsinki Final Act principles guiding participating States;
- the inherent right of all states to choose and to implement freely their own security arrangements, and to be free to choose or change their security arrangements, including treaties of alliance, as they evolve;
- respect for the sovereignty, territorial integrity and political independence of all other states, for the inviolability of frontiers, and the development of good-neighbourly relations;
- the rule of law, the fostering of democracy, political pluralism and a market economy;
- human rights and the rights of persons belonging to national minorities;

- the prevention of conflicts and settlement of disputes by peaceful means in accordance with UN and OSCE principles.
3. Ukraine reaffirms its determination to carry forward its defence reforms, to strengthen democratic and civilian control of the armed forces, and to increase their interoperability with the forces of NATO and Partner countries. NATO reaffirms its support for Ukraine's efforts in these areas.
4. Ukraine welcomes NATO's continuing and active adaptation to meet the changing circumstances of Euro-Atlantic security, and its role, in cooperation with other international organizations such as the OSCE, the European Union, the Council of Europe and the Western European Union in promoting Euro-Atlantic security and fostering a general climate of trust and confidence in Europe.

III. Areas for Consultation and/or Cooperation between NATO and Ukraine

5. Reaffirming the common goal of implementation of a broad range of issues for consultation and cooperation, NATO and Ukraine commit themselves to develop and strengthen their consultation and/or cooperation in the areas described below. In this regard, NATO and Ukraine reaffirm their commitment to the full development of the EAPC and the enhanced PfP. This includes Ukrainian participation in operations, including peacekeeping operations, on a case-by-case basis, under the authority of the UN Security Council, or the responsibility of the OSCE, and, if CJTF are used in such cases, Ukrainian participation in them at an early stage on a case-by-case basis, subject to decisions by the North Atlantic Council on specific operations.
6. Consultations between NATO and Ukraine will cover issues of common concern, such as:
   - political and security related subjects, in particular the development of Euro-Atlantic security and stability, including the security of Ukraine;
   - conflict prevention, crisis management, peace support, conflict resolution and humanitarian operations, taking into account the roles of the United Nations and the OSCE in this field;
   - the political and defence aspects of nuclear, biological and chemical non-proliferation;
   - disarmament and arms control issues, including those related to the Treaty on Conventional Armed Forces in Europe (CFE Treaty), the Open Skies Treaty and confidence and security building measures in the 1994 Vienna Document;
   - arms exports and related technology transfers;
   - combatting drug-trafficking and terrorism.

Areas for consultation and cooperation, in particular through joint seminars, joint working groups, and other cooperative programmes, will cover a broad range of topics, such as:
- civil emergency planning, and disaster preparedness;
- civil-military relations, democratic control of the armed forces, and Ukrainian defence reform;
- defence planning, budgeting, policy, strategy and national security concepts;
- defence conversion;
- NATO-Ukraine military cooperation and interoperability;
- economic aspects of security;
- science and technology issues;
- environmental security issues, including nuclear safety;
- aerospace research and development, through AGARD;
- civil-military coordination of air traffic management and control.

In addition, NATO and Ukraine will explore to the broadest possible degree the following areas for cooperation:
- armaments cooperation (beyond the existing CNAD dialogue);
- military training, including PfP exercises on Ukrainian territory and NATO support for the Polish-Ukrainian peacekeeping battalion;
- promotion of defence cooperation between Ukraine and its neighbours.

Other areas for consultation and cooperation may be added, by mutual agreement, on the basis of experience gained.

Given the importance of information activities to improve reciprocal knowledge and understanding, NATO has established an Information and Documentation Centre in Kyiv. The Ukrainian side will provide its full support to the operation of the Centre in accordance with the Memorandum of Understanding between NATO and the Government of Ukraine signed at Kyiv on 7 May 1997.

IV. Practical Arrangements for Consultation and Cooperation between NATO and Ukraine

11. Consultation and cooperation as set out in this Charter will be implemented through:
    - NATO-Ukraine meetings at the level of the North Atlantic Council at intervals to be mutually agreed;
    - NATO-Ukraine meetings with appropriate NATO Committees as mutually agreed;
    - reciprocal high level visits;
    - mechanisms for military cooperation, including periodic meetings with NATO Chiefs of Defence and activities within the framework of the enhanced Partnership for Peace programme;

- a military liaison mission of Ukraine will be established as part of a Ukrainian mission to NATO in Brussels. NATO retains the right reciprocally to establish a NATO military liaison mission in Kyiv.

Meetings will normally take place at NATO Headquarters in Brussels. Under exceptional circumstances, they may be convened elsewhere, including in Ukraine, as mutually agreed. Meetings, as a rule, will take place on the basis of an agreed calendar.

12. NATO and Ukraine consider their relationship as an evolving, dynamic process. To ensure that they are developing their relationship and implementing the provisions of this Charter to the fullest extent possible, the North Atlantic Council will periodically meet with Ukraine as the NATO-Ukraine Commission, as a rule not less than twice a year. The NATO-Ukraine Commission will not duplicate the functions of other mechanisms described in this Charter, but instead would meet to assess broadly the implementation of the relationship, survey planning for the future, and suggest ways to improve or further develop cooperation between NATO and Ukraine.

13. NATO and Ukraine will encourage expanded dialogue and cooperation between the North Atlantic Assembly and the Verkhovna Rada.

V. Cooperation for a More Secure Europe

14. NATO Allies will continue to support Ukrainian sovereignty and independence, territorial integrity, democratic development, economic prosperity and its status as a non-nuclear weapon state, and the principle of inviolability of frontiers, as key factors of stability and security in Central and Eastern Europe and in the continent as a whole.

15. NATO and Ukraine will develop a crisis consultative mechanism to consult together whenever Ukraine perceives a direct threat to its territorial integrity, political independence, or security.

16. NATO welcomes and supports the fact that Ukraine received security assurances from all five nuclear-weapon states parties to the Treaty on the Non-Proliferation of Nuclear Weapons (NPT) as a non-nuclear weapon state party to the NPT, and recalls the commitments undertaken by the United States and the United Kingdom, together with Russia, and by France unilaterally, which took the historic decision in Budapest in 1994 to provide Ukraine with security assurances as a non-nuclear weapon state party to the NPT.

Ukraine's landmark decision to renounce nuclear weapons and to accede to the NPT as a non-nuclear weapon state greatly contributed to the strengthening of security and stability in Europe and has earned Ukraine special stature in the world community. NATO welcomes Ukraine's decision to support the indefinite extension of the NPT and its contribution to the withdrawal and dismantlement of nuclear weapons which were based on its territory.

Ukraine's strengthened cooperation with NATO will enhance and deepen the political dialogue between Ukraine and the members of the Alliance on a broad range of security matters, including on nuclear issues. This will contribute to the improvement of the overall security environment in Europe.

17. NATO and Ukraine note the entry into force of the CFE Flank Document on 15 May 1997. NATO and Ukraine will continue to cooperate on issues of mutual interest such as CFE adaptation. NATO and Ukraine intend to improve the operation of the CFE treaty in a changing environment and, through that, the security of each state party, irrespective of whether it belongs to a political-military alliance. They share the view that the presence of foreign troops on the territory of a participating state must be in conformity with international law, the freely expressed consent of the host state or a relevant decision of the United Nations Security Council.

18. Ukraine welcomes the statement by NATO members that "enlarging the Alliance will not require a change in NATO's current nuclear posture and, therefore, NATO countries have no intention, no plan and no reason to deploy nuclear weapons on the territory of new members nor any need to change any aspect of NATO's nuclear posture or nuclear policy—and do not foresee any future need to do so."

19. NATO member States and Ukraine will continue fully to implement all agreements on disarmament, non-proliferation and arms control and confidence-building measures they are part of.

The present Charter takes effect upon its signature.

The present Charter is established in two originals in the English, French and Ukrainian languages, all three texts having equal validity.

NATO-Russia Relations: A New Quality Declaration by Heads of State and Government of NATO Member States and the Russian Federation

At the start of the 21st century we live in a new, closely interrelated world, in which unprecedented new threats and challenges demand increasingly united responses. Consequently, we, the member states of the North Atlantic Treaty Organization and the Russian Federation are today opening a new page in our relations, aimed at enhancing our ability to work together in areas of common interest and to stand together against common threats and risks to our security. As participants of the Founding Act on Mutual Relations, Cooperation and Security, we reaffirm the goals, principles and commitments set forth therein, in particular our determination to build together a lasting and inclusive peace in the Euro-Atlantic area on the principles of democracy and cooperative security and the principle that the security of all states in the Euro-Atlantic community is indivisible. We are convinced that a qualitatively new relationship between NATO and the Russian Federation will constitute an essential contribution in achieving this goal. In this context, we will observe in good faith our obligations under international law, including the UN Charter, provisions and principles contained in the Helsinki Final Act and the OSCE Charter for European Security.

Building on the Founding Act and taking into account the initiative taken by our Foreign Ministers, as reflected in their statement of 7 December 2001, to bring together NATO member states and Russia to identify and pursue opportunities for joint action at twenty, we hereby establish the NATO-Russia Council. In the framework of the NATO-Russia Council, NATO member states and Russia will work as equal partners in areas of common interest. The NATO-Russia Council will provide a mechanism for consultation, consensus-building, cooperation, joint decision, and joint action for the member states of NATO and Russia on a wide spectrum of security issues in the Euro-Atlantic region.

The NATO-Russia Council will serve as the principal structure and venue for advancing the relationship between NATO and Russia. It will operate on the principle of consensus. It will work on the basis of a continuous political dialogue on security issues among its members with a view to early identification of emerging problems, determination of optimal common approaches and the conduct of joint actions, as appropriate. The members of the NATO-Russia Council, acting in their national capacities and in a manner consistent with their respective collective commitments and obligations, will take joint decisions and will bear equal responsibility, individually and jointly, for their implementation. Each member may raise in the NATO-Russia Council issues related to the implementation of joint decisions.

The NATO-Russia Council will be chaired by the Secretary General of NATO. It will meet at the level of Foreign Ministers and at the level of Defence Ministers twice annually, and at the level of Heads of State and Government as appropriate. Meetings of the Council at Ambassadorial level will be held at least once a month, with the possibility of more frequent meetings as needed, including extraordinary meetings, which will take place at the request of any Member or the NATO Secretary General.

To support and prepare the meetings of the Council a Preparatory Committee is established, at the level of the NATO Political Committee, with Russian representation at the appropriate level. The Preparatory Committee will meet twice monthly, or more often if necessary. The NATO-Russia Council may also establish committees or working groups for individual subjects or areas of cooperation on an ad hoc or permanent basis, as appropriate. Such committees and working groups will draw upon the resources of existing NATO committees.

Under the auspices of the Council, military representatives and Chiefs of Staff will also meet. Meetings of Chiefs of Staff will take place no less than twice a year, meetings at military representatives level at least once a month, with the possibility of more frequent meetings as needed. Meetings of military experts may be convened as appropriate.

The NATO-Russia Council, replacing the NATO-Russia Permanent Joint Council, will focus on all areas of mutual interest identified in Section III of the Founding Act, including the provision to add other areas by mutual agreement. The work programmes for 2002 agreed in December 2001 for the PJC and its subordinate bodies will continue to be implemented under the auspices and rules of the NATO-Russia Council. NATO member states and Russia will continue to intensify their cooperation in areas including the struggle against terrorism, crisis management, non-proliferation, arms control and confidence-building measures, theatre missile defence, search and rescue at sea, military-to-military cooperation, and civil emergencies. This cooperation may complement cooperation in other fora. As initial steps in this regard, we have today agreed to pursue the following cooperative efforts:

- **Struggle Against Terrorism:** strengthen cooperation through a multi-faceted approach, including joint assessments of the terrorist threat to the Euro-Atlantic area, focused on specific threats, for example, to Russian and NATO forces, to civilian aircraft, or to critical infrastructure; an initial step will be a joint assessment of the terrorist threat to NATO, Russia and Partner peacekeeping forces in the Balkans.
- **Crisis Management:** strengthen cooperation, including through: regular exchanges of views and information on peacekeeping operations, including continuing cooperation and consultations on the situation in the Balkans; promoting interoperability between national peacekeeping contingents, including through joint or coordinated training initiatives; and further development of a generic concept for joint NATO-Russia peacekeeping operations.
- **Non-Proliferation:** broaden and strengthen cooperation against the proliferation of weapons of mass destruction (WMD) and the means of their delivery, and contribute to strengthening existing non-proliferation arrangements through: a structured exchange of views, leading to a joint assessment of global trends in proliferation of nuclear, biological and chemical agents; and exchange of experience with the goal of exploring opportunities for intensified practical cooperation on protection from nuclear, biological and chemical agents.
- **Arms Control and Confidence-Building Measures:** recalling the contributions of arms control and confidence—and security-building measures (CSBMs) to stability in the Euro-Atlantic area and reaffirming adherence to the Treaty on Conventional Armed Forces in Europe (CFE) as a cornerstone of European security, work cooperatively toward ratification by all the States Parties and entry into force of the Agreement on Adaptation of the CFE Treaty, which would permit accession by non-CFE states; continue consultations on the CFE and Open Skies Treaties; and continue the NATO-Russia nuclear experts consultations.
- **Theatre Missile Defence:** enhance consultations on theatre missile defence (TMD), in particular on TMD concepts, terminology, systems and system capabilities, to analyse and evaluate possible levels of interoperability among respective TMD systems, and explore opportunities for intensified practical cooperation, including joint training and exercises.
- **Search and Rescue at Sea:** monitor the implementation of the NATO-Russia Framework Document on Submarine Crew Rescue, and continue

to promote cooperation, transparency and confidence between NATO and Russia in the area of search and rescue at sea.

- **Military-to-Military Cooperation and Defence Reform:** pursue enhanced military-to-military cooperation and interoperability through enhanced joint training and exercises and the conduct of joint demonstrations and tests; explore the possibility of establishing an integrated NATO-Russia military training centre for missions to address the challenges of the 21st century; enhance cooperation on defence reform and its economic aspects, including conversion.

- **Civil Emergencies:** pursue enhanced mechanisms for future NATO-Russia cooperation in responding to civil emergencies. Initial steps will include the exchange of information on recent disasters and the exchange of WMD consequence management information.

- **New Threats and Challenges:** In addition to the areas enumerated above, explore possibilities for confronting new challenges and threats to the Euro-Atlantic area in the framework of the activities of the NATO Committee on Challenges to Modern Society (CCMS); initiate cooperation in the field of civil and military airspace controls; and pursue enhanced scientific cooperation.

The members of the NATO-Russia Council will work with a view to identifying further areas of cooperation.

Partnership with the countries of Central and Eastern Europe (statement issued by the North Atlantic Council meeting in Ministerial Session)

Copenhagen, 7 June 1991

1. The long decades of European division are over. We welcome the major increase in the contacts by the Alliance and its members with the Soviet Union and the other countries of Central and Eastern Europe, as they accept the hand of friendship extended by Alliance Heads of States and Government in London last year. We welcome the progress made by the peoples of these countries towards political and economic reform. We seek to build constructive partnerships with them in order further to promote security and stability in a free and undivided Europe which will recognise the political, economic, social and ecological elements of security, along with the indispensable defence dimension. President Gorbachev's Nobel lecture in Oslo yesterday strengthens our belief that this objective is within reach.

2. The changes that have occurred in Europe since 1989 have substantially increased the security of all European states. We have seen the end of East-West antagonism, progress towards democracy, major achievements in arms control, the adoption of the Charter of Paris and the signature of a Joint Declaration of 22 States, whose continuing importance we underline. We note, however, that concerns about security remain in some countries.

3. Our own security is inseparably linked to that of all other states in Europe. The consolidation and preservation throughout the continent of democratic societies and their freedom from any form of coercion or intimidation are therefore of direct and material concern to us, as they are to all other CSCE states under the commitments of the Helsinki Final Act and the Charter of Paris. Our common security can best be safeguarded through the further development of a network of interlocking institutions and relationships, constituting a comprehensive architecture in which the Alliance, the process of European integration and the CSCE are key elements. Emerging frame-works of regional cooperation will also be

important. Consistent with the purely defensive nature of our Alliance, we will neither seek unilateral advantage from the changed situation in Europe nor threaten the legitimate interests of any state, but rather pursue our efforts to ensure that all peoples of Europe can live in peace and security. We do not wish to isolate any country, nor to see a new division of the Continent. Our objective is to help create a Europe whole and free.

4. The CSCE process—and its institutions created in Paris last November—play a central role in expanding the network of cooperative relationships across Europe. It provides a framework within which we will actively seek, as individual Allies and through institutions, including the European Community and the Council of Europe, the development of closer relations with the states of Central and Eastern Europe as they pursue their democratic development. The Allies have a clear interest in the observance of the principles and provision of the Helsinki Final Act and the Charter of Paris. We remain fully committed to the CSCE as a political process. We have played a key role in its development, and our consultations within the Alliance continue to be a source of initiatives for strengthening CSCE.

5. We are committed to work with the other CSCE participating states in making the forthcoming meeting of Foreign Ministers in Berlin a decisive new step in reinforcing CSCE's role and in consolidating its new institutional component, especially by enhancing its capacity for political consultation. In particular, we will seek to reinforce the CSCE's potential for conflict prevention, crisis management and the peaceful settlement of disputes by appropriate means, such as creating a suitably structured emergency consultation mechanism and strengthening the Conflict Prevention centre. We seek an architecture for the new Europe that is firmly based on the principles and provisions of the Helsinki Final Act and the Charter of Paris.

6. We will continue with all available means to support reforms undertaken in the Central and Eastern European states to establish democratic systems of government based on the rule of law and the respect for human rights, as well as the related efforts to create modern competitive market-oriented economies. We are convinced that, notwithstanding present transnational hardships, its is only on those foundations of political and economic freedom that the legitimate aspirations of peoples of those states can be met and grave economic disparities increasingly overcome. We support also the wide range of bilateral and regional contacts, treaties and programmes which are developing between our countries and those

of Central and Eastern Europe, as well as positive developments in relations between those countries.

7. We reaffirm our wish to see difficulties accompanying political and economic reform in these countries resolved in a peaceful manner and to satisfaction of all concerned. In this context, we support the expectations and legitimate aspirations of the Baltic peoples. We call on the Soviet authorities to continue to seek through dialogue and genuine negotiations with the democratically elected leaders of the three Baltic republics a negotiated solution based on the principles of the Helsinki Final Act, and on all concerned to exercise restraint.

8. In the context of the developing network of European security relationships, we welcome the success of the initiative by the Alliance Heads of State and Government last year in London to establish regular diplomatic liaison with the states of Central and Eastern Europe. It has proved its value in fostering new patterns of constructive dialogue and bonds of friendship. President Havel's recent meeting with the North Atlantic Council was an important symbol of the new undivided Europe that is emerging. We look forward to future visits by the leaders of the Soviet Union and the other Central and Eastern European States. To ensure full mutual understanding of legitimate security interests and policies, we intend to develop further our regular diplomatic liaison along the lines foreseen in the London Declaration in fields of interest to the Alliance and its new partners and also to intensify our programme of military contacts at various levels. These efforts underscore our intention to contribute to the development of peaceful and friendly international relations, consistent with the spirit of Article 2 of the Treaty of Washington.

9. We see the strengthening of our relations with these countries as a process over time, designed to promote both mutual reassurance and increasingly close ties. In doing so, the Alliance will contribute to the achievement of the objectives of the CSCE while preserving its responsibilities and mechanisms. While pursuing our present programme of highranking political visits and regular diplomatic liaison, we are determined to make the best possible use of our resources to give expression to our commitment to an evolving security partnership through the implementation of a broad set of further initiatives, including:

- The organisation of meetings of officials and experts to exchange views and information on security policy issues, on military strategy and doctrine and on other current topics in the security files, such as exchange of experience in the domain of arms control, and non-proliferation and the conversion of defence industries to civilian purposes.

- Intensified military contacts between senior NATO military authorities and their counterparts in the Central and East European states, discussion at NATO Headquarters, SHAPE and major NATO commands with military officers from those countries on matters of mutual concern, and invitations to military training facilities for special familiarisation programmes, including issues connected to civilian oversight of defence.
- Participation of Central and East European experts in certain Alliance activities, including those related to NATO's "Third Dimension" scientific and environmental programmes, and exchange of views on subjects such as airspace management.
- Gradual expansion of NATO's information programmes in the region, support for discussion of security issues in a democratic context within those countries and invitations to parliamentary, educational and media groups and delegations of young leaders to visit NATO Headquarters.
- Encouragement of greater contacts between Central and East European parliaments and the North Atlantic Assembly, to be agreed among the parliamentarians concerned.

10. On this basis, we are determined that our Alliance shall make its full contribution to the building of stable and durable peace and security in all countries of Europe. We invite all European states to join with us in realising this shared objective.

Declaration on Peace and Cooperation issued by the Heads of State and Government participating in the meeting of the North Atlantic Council (including decisions leading to the creation of the North Atlantic Cooperation Council (NACC)) ("The Rome Declaration")

Rome, 8 November 1991

1. We, the Heads of State and Government of the member countries of the North Atlantic Alliance, have gathered in Rome to open a new chapter in the history of our Alliance. The far-reaching decisions we have taken here mark an important stage in the transformation of NATO that we launched in London last year.

2. The world has changed dramatically. The Alliance has made an essential contribution. The peoples of North America and the whole of Europe can now join in a community of shared values based on freedom, democracy, human rights and the rule of law. As an agent of change, a source of stability and the indispensable guarantor of its members' security, our Alliance will continue to play a key role in building a new, lasting order of peace in Europe: a Europe of cooperation and prosperity.

A new security architecture
3. The challenges we will face in this new Europe cannot be comprehensively addressed by one institution alone, but only in a framework of interlocking institutions tying together the countries of Europe and North America. Consequently, we are working toward a new European security architecture in which NATO, the CSCE, the European Community, the WEU and the Council of Europe complement each other. Regional frame-works of cooperation will also be important. This interaction will be of the greatest significance in preventing

instability and divisions that could result from various causes, such as economic disparities and violent nationalism.

The future role of the Alliance: our new Strategic Concept
4. Yesterday, we published our new Strategic Concept. Our security has substantially improved: we no longer face the old threat of a massive attack. However, prudence requires us to maintain an overall strategic balance and to remain ready to meet any potential risks to our security which may arise from instability or tension. In an environment of uncertainty and unpredictable challenges, our Alliance, which provides the essential transatlantic link as demonstrated by the significant presence of North American forces in Europe, retains its enduring value. Our new strategic concept reaffirms NATO's core functions and allows us, within the radically changed situation in Europe, to realise in full our broad approach to stability and security encompassing political, economic, social and environmental aspects, along with the indispensable defence dimension. Never has the opportunity to achieve our Alliance's objectives by political means, in keeping with Articles 2 and 4 of the Washington Treaty, been greater. Consequently, our security policy can now be based on three mutually reinforcing elements: dialogue; cooperation; and the maintenance of a collective defence capability. The use, as appropriate, of these elements will be particularly important to prevent or manage crises affecting our security.

5. The military dimension of our Alliance remains an essential factor; but what is new is that, more than ever, it will serve a broad concept of security. The Alliance will maintain its purely defensive purpose, its collective arrangements based on an integrated military structure as well as cooperation and coordination agreements, and for the foreseeable future an appropriate mix of conventional and nuclear forces. Our military forces will adjust to their new tasks, becoming smaller and more flexible. Thus, our conventional forces will be substantially reduced as will, in many cases, their readiness. They will also be given increased mobility to enable them to react to a wide range of contingencies, and will be organised for flexible build-up, when necessary, for crisis management as well as defence. Multinational formations will play a greater role within the integrated military structure. Nuclear forces committed to NATO will be greatly reduced: the current NATO stockpile of sub-strategic weapons in Europe will be cut by roughly 80% in accordance with the decisions taken by the Nuclear Planning Group in Taormina. The fundamental purpose of the nuclear forces of the Allies remains political: to preserve peace, and prevent war or any kind of coercion.

European security identity and defence role
6. We reaffirm the consensus expressed by our Ministers of Foreign Affairs in Copenhagen. The development of a European security identity and defence role, reflected in the further strengthening of the European pillar within the Alliance, will reinforce the integrity and effectiveness of the Atlantic Alliance. The enhancement of the role and responsibility of the European members is an important basis for the transformation of the Alliance. These two positive processes are mutually reinforcing. We are agreed, in parallel with the emergence and development of a European security identity and defence role, to enhance the essential transatlantic link that the Alliance guarantees and fully to maintain the strategic unity and indivisibility of security of all our members. The Alliance is the essential forum for consultation among its members and the venue for agreement on policies bearing on the security and defence commitments of Allies under the Washington Treaty. Recognising that it is for the European Allies concerned to decide what arrangements are needed for the expression of a common European foreign and security policy and defence role, we further agree that, as the two processes advance, we will develop practical arrangements to ensure the necessary transparency and complementarity between the European security and defence identity as it emerges in the Twelve and the WEU, and the Alliance.

7. We welcome the spirit in which those Allies who are also members of the Twelve and the WEU have kept the other members of the Alliance informed about the progress of their ongoing discussions on the development of the European identity and about other issues, such as their peace efforts in Yugoslavia. Appropriate links and consultation procedures between the Twelve and the WEU, and the Alliance will be developed in order to ensure that the Allies that are not currently participating in the development of a European identity in foreign and security policy and defence should be adequately involved in decisions that may affect their security. The Alliance's new Strategic Concept, being an agreed conceptual basis for the forces of all Allies, should facilitate the necessary complementarity between the Alliance and the emerging defence component of the European integration process. As the transformation of the Alliance proceeds, we intend to preserve the operational coherence we now have and on which our defence depends. We welcome the perspective of a reinforcement of the role of the WEU, both as the defence component of the process of European unification and as a means of strengthening the European pillar of the Alliance, bearing in mind the different nature of its relations with the Alliance and with the European Political Union.

8. We note the gradual convergence of views in the discussions concerning the developing European security identity and defence role compatible with the common defence policy we already have in our Alliance. We feel confident that in line with the consensus in Copenhagen, the result will contribute to a strong new transatlantic partnership by strengthening the European component in a transformed Alliance. We will help move this development forward.

Relations with the Soviet Union and the other countries of Central and Eastern Europe: A qualitative step forward
9. We have consistently encouraged the development of democracy in the Soviet Union and the other countries of Central and Eastern Europe. We therefore applaud the commitment of these countries to political and economic reform following the rejection of totalitarian communist rule by their peoples. We salute the newly recovered independence of the Baltic States. We will support all steps in the countries of Central and Eastern Europe towards reform and will give practical assistance to help them succeed in this difficult transition. This is based on our conviction that our own security is inseparably linked to that of all other states in Europe.

10. The Alliance can aid in fostering a sense of security and confidence in these countries, thereby strengthening their ability to fulfil their CSCE commitments and make democratic change irrevocable. Wishing to enhance its contribution to the emergence of a Europe whole and free, our Alliance at its London Summit extended to the Central and Eastern European countries the hand of friendship and established regular diplomatic liaison. Together we signed the Paris Joint Declaration. In Copenhagen last June, the Alliance took further initiatives to develop partnership with these countries. Our extensive programme of high level visits, exchanges of views on security and other related issues, intensified military contacts, and exchanges of expertise in various fields has demonstrated its value and contributed greatly to building a new relationship between NATO and these countries. This is a dynamic process: the growth of democratic institutions throughout Central and Eastern Europe and encouraging cooperative experiences, as well as the desire of these countries for closer ties, now call for our relations to be broadened, intensified and raised to a qualitatively new level.

11. Therefore, as the next step, we intend to develop a more institutional relationship of consultation and cooperation on political and security issues. We invite, at this stage of the process, the Foreign Ministers of the Republic of Bulgaria, the Czech and Slovak Federal Republic, the Republic of Estonia, the Republic of Hungary, the Republic of Latvia, the Republic of Lithuania, the

Republic of Poland, the Republic of Romania, and the Soviet Union to join our Foreign Ministers in December 1991 in Brussels to issue a joint political declaration to launch this new era of partnership and to define further the modalities and content of this process. In particular, we propose the following activities:

- annual meetings with the North Atlantic Council at Ministerial level in what might be called a North Atlantic Cooperation Council;
- periodic meetings with the North Atlantic Council at Ambassadorial level;
- additional meetings with the North Atlantic Council at Ministerial or Ambassadorial level as circumstances warrant;
- regular meetings, at intervals to be mutually agreed, with:
  - NATO subordinate committees, including the Political and Economic Committees;
  - the Military Committee and under its direction other NATO Military Authorities.

This process will contribute to the achievement of the objectives of the CSCE without prejudice to its competence and mechanisms. It will be carried out in accordance with the core functions of the Alliance.

12. Our consultations and cooperation will focus on security and related issues where Allies can offer their experience and expertise, such as defence planning, democratic concepts of civilian-military relations, civil-military coordination of air traffic management, and the conversion of defence production to civilian purposes. Our new initiative will enhance participation of our partners in the "Third Dimension" of scientific and environmental programmes of our Alliance. It will also allow the widest possible dissemination of information about NATO in the Central and Eastern European countries, inter alia through diplomatic liaison channels and our embassies. We will provide the appropriate resources to support our liaison activities.

The conference on security and cooperation in Europe
13. We remain deeply committed to strengthening the CSCE process, which has a vital role to play in promoting stability and democracy in Europe in a period of historic change. We will intensify our efforts to enhance the CSCE's role, in the first instance by working with the other participating CSCE states to ensure that the Helsinki Follow-Up Meeting in 1992 will be another major step towards building a new Europe. The CSCE has the outstanding advantage of being the only forum that brings together all countries of Europe and Canada and the United States under a common code of human rights, fundamental freedoms, democracy, rule of law, security, and economic liberty. The new CSCE institutions and structures,

which we proposed at our London Summit and which were created at the Paris Summit, must be consolidated and further developed so as to provide CSCE with the means to help ensure full implementation of the Helsinki Final Act, the Charter of Paris, and other relevant CSCE documents and thus permit the CSCE to meet the new challenges which Europe will have to face. Our consultations within the Alliance continue to be a source of initiatives for strengthening the CSCE.

14. Consequently, we will actively support the development of the CSCE to enhance its capacity as the organ for consultation and cooperation among all participating States, capable of effective action in line with its new and increased responsibilities, in particular on the questions of human rights and security including arms control and disarmament, and for effective crisis management and peaceful settlement of disputes, consistent with international law and CSCE principles. To this end, we suggest:

- that the CSCE Council, the central forum for political consultations, continue to take decisions on questions relating to the CSCE and the functions and structures of the CSCE institutions;
- that the Committee of Senior Officials serve as the coordination and management body between Council sessions and that it acquire a greater operational capacity and meet more frequently, with a view to ensuring the implementation of decisions;
- that the CSCE's conflict prevention and crisis management capabilities be improved: as one contribution, in addition to the functions entrusted to it by the Paris Charter, the means available to the Conflict Prevention Centre should be strengthened and made more flexible to enable it to fulfil the specific tasks assigned to it by the CSCE Council and the Committee of Senior Officials;
- that specific tasks based on a precise mandate by the CSCE Council or the Committee of Senior Officials might be entrusted to ad hoc groups;
- that the decisions taken at the Helsinki Follow-Up Meeting ensure complementarity among CSCE activities in the security field including, inter alia, conflict prevention, arms control and consultations on security;
- that consideration should be given within the CSCE to develop further the CSCE's capability to safeguard, through peaceful means, human rights, democracy and the rule of law in cases of clear, gross and uncorrected violations of relevant CSCE commitments, if necessary in the absence of the consent of the state concerned;
- that the Office for Free Elections be transformed into a broadly focused Office of Democratic Institutions to promote cooperation in the fields of human rights, democracy and the rule of law;

- that the monitoring and promotion of progress on human dimension issues be continued in the form of periodic meetings of short duration on clearly defined issues;
- that further political impetus be given to economic, scientific and environmental cooperation so as to promote the basis of prosperity for stable, democratic development.

Arms Control

15. We strongly support President Bush's initiative of 27 September 1991 which has opened new prospects for nuclear arms reduction. We also welcome President Gorbachev's response. We particularly applaud the decision of both sides to eliminate their nuclear warheads for ground-launched shortrange weapons systems. The Allies concerned, through their consultations, have played a central role in President Bush's decision which fulfilled the SNF arms control objectives of the London Declaration. They will continue close consultations on the process of the elimination of ground-based SNF warheads until its completion. We will continue to work for security at minimum levels of nuclear arms sufficient to preserve peace and stability. We look forward to the early ratification of the recently signed START agreement.

16. We note with satisfaction the recent achievements in the fields of conventional arms control and disarmament. We reiterate the paramount importance we attach to the CFE Treaty and call upon all CFE signatories to move forward promptly with its ratification and implementation. We urge our negotiating partners to work with us to reach substantial agreements in the CFE IA and CSBM negotiations, and remain dedicated to achieving concrete results by the time of the CSCE Helsinki Follow-Up Meeting. We welcome the resumption of the Open Skies negotiations; we look forward to agreement on an Open Skies regime by the time of the Helsinki Meeting as an important new element in greater openness and confidence-building in the military field.

17. The Helsinki Meeting will mark a turning point in the arms control and disarmament process in Europe, now with the participation of all CSCE states. This will offer a unique opportunity to move this process energetically forward. Our goal will be to shape a new cooperative order, in which no country needs to harbour fears for its security, by:

- strengthening security and stability at lower levels of armed forces to the extent possible and commensurate with individual legitimate security needs both inside and outside of Europe;

- conducting an intensified security dialogue within a permanent framework and fostering a new quality of transparency and cooperation about armed forces and defence policies; and
- promoting effective mechanisms and instruments for conflict prevention.

18. The proliferation of weapons of mass destruction and of their means of delivery undermines international security. Transfers of conventional armaments beyond legitimate defensive needs to regions of tension make the peaceful settlement of disputes less likely. We support the establishment by the United Nations of a universal non-discriminatory register of conventional arms transfers. We support steps undertaken to address other aspects of proliferation and other initiatives designed to build confidence and underpin international security. We also deem it essential to complete a global, comprehensive and effectively verifiable ban on chemical weapons next year. We welcome the positive results of the Third Review Conference of the Biological and Toxin Weapons Convention, in particular the decision to explore the feasibility of verification.

Broader Challenges

19. Our Strategic Concept underlines that Alliance security must take account of the global context. It points out risks of a wider nature, including proliferation of weapons of mass destruction, disruption of the flow of vital resources and actions of terrorism and sabotage, which can affect Alliance security interests. We reaffirm the importance of arrangements existing in the Alliance for consultation among the Allies under Article 4 of the Washington Treaty and, where appropriate, coordination of our efforts including our responses to such risks. We will continue to address broader challenges in our consultations and in the appropriate multilateral forums in the widest possible cooperation with other states.

20. The North Atlantic Alliance was founded with two purposes: the defence of the territory of its members, and the safeguarding and promotion of the values they share. In a still uncertain world, the need for defence remains. But in a world where the values which we uphold are shared ever more widely, we gladly seize the opportunity to adapt our defences accordingly; to cooperate and consult with our new partners; to help consolidate a now undivided continent of Europe; and to make our Alliance's contribution to a new age of confidence, stability and peace.

21. We express our deep appreciation for the gracious hospitality extended to us by the Government of the Italian Republic.

Study on NATO Enlargement

Contents

Chapter 1*: Purposes and Principles of Enlargement*

A. Purposes of Enlargement

1. With the end of the Cold War, there is a unique opportunity to build an improved security architecture in the whole of the Euro-Atlantic area. The aim of an improved security architecture is to provide increased stability and security for all in the Euro-Atlantic area, without recreating dividing lines. NATO views security as a broad concept embracing political and economic, as well as defence, components. Such a broad concept of security should be the basis for the new security architecture which must be built through a gradual process of integration and cooperation brought about by an interplay of existing multilateral institutions in Europe, such as the EU, WEU and OSCE, each of which would have a role to play in accordance with its respective responsibilities and purposes in implementing this broad security concept. In this process, which is already well under way, the Alliance has played and will play a strong, active and essential role as one of the cornerstones of stability and security in Europe. NATO remains a purely defensive Alliance whose fundamental purpose is to preserve peace in the Euro-Atlantic area and to provide security for its members.

2. When NATO invites other European countries to become Allies, as foreseen in Article 10 of the Washington Treaty and reaffirmed at the January 1994 Brussels Summit, this will be a further step towards the Alliance's basic goal of enhancing security and stability throughout the Euro-Atlantic area, within the context of a broad European security architecture. NATO enlargement will extend to new members the benefits of common defence and integration into European and Euro-Atlantic institutions. The benefits of common defence and such integration are important to protecting the further democratic development of new members. By integrating more countries into the existing community of values and institutions, consistent with the objectives of the Washington Treaty and the London Declaration, NATO enlargement will safeguard the freedom and security of all its members in accordance with the principles of the UN Charter. Meeting NATO's

fundamental security goals and supporting the integration of new members into European and Euro-Atlantic institutions are thus complementary goals of the enlargement process, consistent with the Alliance's strategic concept.

3. Therefore, enlargement will contribute to enhanced stability and security for all countries in the Euro-Atlantic area by:
   - Encouraging and supporting democratic reforms, including civilian and democratic control over the military;
   - Fostering in new members of the Alliance the patterns and habits of cooperation, consultation and consensus building which characterize relations among current Allies;
   - Promoting good-neighbourly relations, which would benefit all countries in the Euro-Atlantic area, both members and non-members of NATO;
   - Emphasizing common defence and extending its benefits and increasing transparency in defence planning and military budgets, thereby reducing the likelihood of instability that might be engendered by an exclusively national approach to defence policies;
   - Reinforcing the tendency toward integration and cooperation in Europe based on shared democratic values and thereby curbing the countervailing tendency towards disintegration along ethnic and territorial lines;
   - Strengthening the Alliance's ability to contribute to European and international security, including through peacekeeping activities under the responsibility of the OSCE and peacekeeping operations under the authority of the UN Security Council as well as other new missions;
   - Strengthening and broadening the Trans-Atlantic partnership.

B. Principles of enlargement

4. Enlargement of the Alliance will be through accession of new member states to the Washington Treaty. Enlargement should:
   - Accord with, and help to promote, the purposes and principles of the Charter of the United Nations, and the safeguarding of the freedom, common heritage and civilisation of all Alliance members and their people, founded on the principles of democracy, individual liberty and the rule of law. New members will need to conform to these basic principles;

- Accord strictly with Article 10 of the Washington Treaty which states that *"the parties may, by unanimous agreement, invite any other European state in a position to further the principles of this Treaty and to contribute to the security of the North Atlantic area to accede to this Treaty..."*;
- Be on the basis that new members will enjoy all the rights and assume all obligations of membership under the Washington Treaty; and accept and conform with the principles, policies and procedures adopted by all members of the Alliance at the time that new members join;
- Strengthen the Alliance's effectiveness and cohesion; and preserve the Alliance's political and military capability to perform its core functions of common defence as well as to undertake peacekeeping and other new missions;
- Be part of a broad European security architecture based on true cooperation throughout the whole of Europe. It would threaten no-one; and enhance stability and security for all of Europe;
- Take account of the continuing important role of PfP, which will both help prepare interested partners, through their participation in PfP activities, for the benefits and responsibilities of eventual membership and serve as a means to strengthen relations with partner countries which may be unlikely to join the Alliance early or at all. Active participation in the Partnership for Peace will play an important role in the evolutionary process of the enlargement of NATO;
- Complement the enlargement of the European Union, a parallel process which also, for its part, contributes significantly to extending security and stability to the new democracies in the East.

5. New members, at the time that they join, must commit themselves, as all current Allies do on the basis of the Washington Treaty, to:
   - unite their efforts for collective defence and for the preservation of peace and security; settle any international disputes in which they may be involved by peaceful means in such a manner that international peace and security and justice are not endangered, and refrain in their international relations from the threat or use of force in any manner inconsistent with the purposes of the United Nations;
   - contribute to the development of peaceful and friendly international relations by strengthening their free institutions, by bringing about a better understanding of the principles upon which these institutions are founded, and by promoting conditions of stability and well-being;

- maintain the effectiveness of the Alliance by sharing roles, risks, responsibilities, costs and benefits of assuring common security goals and objectives.

6. States which have ethnic disputes or external territorial disputes, including irredentist claims, or internal jurisdictional disputes must settle those disputes by peaceful means in accordance with OSCE principles. Resolution of such disputes would be a factor in determining whether to invite a state to join the Alliance.

7. Decisions on enlargement will be for NATO itself. Enlargement will occur through a gradual, deliberate, and transparent process, encompassing dialogue with all interested parties. There is no fixed or rigid list of criteria for inviting new member states to join the Alliance. Enlargement will be decided on a case-by-case basis and some nations may attain membership before others. New members should not be admitted or excluded on the basis of belonging to some group or category. Ultimately, Allies will decide by consensus whether to invite each new member to join according to their judgment of whether doing so will contribute to security and stability in the North Atlantic area at the time such a decision is to be made. NATO enlargement would proceed in accordance with the provisions of the various OSCE documents which confirm the sovereign right of each state to freely seek its own security arrangements, to belong or not to belong to international organisations, including treaties of alliance. No country outside the Alliance should be given a veto or droit de regard over the process and decisions.

8. NATO's collective defence arrangements, as described in paragraphs 47 and 48, are a concrete expression of Allies' commitment to maintain and develop their individual and collective capacity to resist armed attack. Against the background of existing arrangements for contributing to collective defence, Allies will want to know how possible new members intend to contribute to NATO's collective defence and will explore all aspects of this question in detail through bilateral dialogue prior to accession negotiations.

Chapter 2: *How to ensure that enlargement contributes to the stability and security of the entire Euro-Atlantic area, as part of a broad European security architecture, and supports the objective of an undivided Europe*

A. Introduction—NATO Enlargement in its Broad Context

9. NATO plays an essential role within the developing European Security Architecture. NATO's membership of like-minded Allies dedicated to

working together has, over the course of its forty-five year existence, helped fundamentally improve the nature of relations between member states. Moreover, the commitment by all Allies to defend one another's territory has proven its value, over more than four decades, as an anchor of stability and confidence in Europe. This commitment has helped Allied countries develop powerful and flexible military capabilities, firmly under political control. NATO's reliance on collective defence has ensured that no single Ally is forced to rely upon its own national efforts alone in dealing with basic security challenges. Sharing these benefits with new members can help extend security and stability in Europe. NATO's enlargement will occur as one element of the broader evolution of European cooperation and security currently underway. NATO's enlargement must be understood as only one important element of a broad European security architecture that transcends and renders obsolete the idea of *"dividing lines"* in Europe.

10. The current discussion on enlargement is taking place in very different circumstances than those which prevailed during the Cold War. In this context, the decision to admit new members must reflect the fact that the security challenges and risks which NATO faces now are different in nature from those faced in the past. In 1991, the Strategic Concept stated, *"The threat of a simultaneous, full-scale attack on all of NATO's European fronts has effectively been removed...."*. Since then, the risk of a re-emergent large-scale military threat has further declined. Nevertheless, risks to European security remain, which are multi-faceted and multi-directional and thus hard to predict and assess. NATO must be capable of responding to such risks and new challenges as they develop if stability in Europe and the security of its members, old and new, are to be preserved. For their part, numerous countries aspire to NATO membership in the wider context of becoming part of existing European and Euro-Atlantic structures and strengthening their security and stability.

11. Stability and security in Europe will be strengthened through an evolutionary process, taking into account political and security developments in the whole of Europe. NATO enlargement will be part of that process, threaten no-one and contribute to a developing broad European security architecture based on true cooperation throughout the whole of Europe, enhancing stability and security for all.

12. The architecture of European security is composed of European institutions (such as the European Union (EU) and the Western European Union (WEU)) and transatlantic institutions (NATO). It also includes

the OSCE, whose membership comprises all European as well as North American countries and is thus the most inclusive European security institution, in whose framework agreements of particular importance for European security (the CFE Treaty and the Pact on Stability) have been concluded. For its part, NATO has developed cooperation arrangements: the NACC and PfP. NACC/PfP cooperation will continue to play an important role in the European security architecture both in enlarging the Alliance and in strengthening Alliance relations with partner countries which may not join the Alliance early or at all. This is addressed in Chapter 3.

13. Enlargement will have implications for all European nations, including states which do not join NATO early or at all. It will be important to maintain active, cooperative relations with countries which do not join the Alliance, in order to avoid divisions or uncertainties in Europe and to ensure broad, inclusive approaches to cooperative security. The Alliance should underline that there can be no question of *"spheres of influence"* in the contemporary Europe. NATO's relations with other European states, whether cooperation partners or not, are important factors to consider in taking any decision to proceed with the enlargement process as is building security for states which may not be prospective NATO members. Any such decision will have a significant impact on the European security environment and its timing, therefore, will require careful consideration. Implementation of Russia's Individual Partnership Programme under the PfP and of our dialogue and cooperation with Russia beyond PfP will together renew and extend cooperation between the Alliance and Russia which we believe will enhance stability and security in Europe, as part of our broad approach to developing a cooperative security architecture in Europe. Equally, we want to develop further our relations with all newly independent states, whose independence and democracy constitute an important factor of security and stability for Europe. In this context, we attach particular importance to our relations with Ukraine which we will further develop, especially through enhanced cooperation within the PfP.

B. NATO Enlargement and Other European Security Institutions, in particular the OSCE, EU and WEU

14. There are several institutions with a critical role to play in the emerging European security architecture. It is important to assess NATO's enlargement in terms of how it can contribute to stability and security in conjunction with these other institutions.

15. As the most inclusive institution in the European security architecture, the OSCE has a key role to play in maintaining security and transcending divisions in Europe and should continue to be strengthened independently of enlargement of NATO. A strengthened OSCE will help to provide reassurance to states which may not join NATO either early or at all. The OSCE has developed unique capabilities in its 20-year history to contribute to security and stability in such areas as early warning, conflict prevention and crisis management, confidence and security-building measures, economic cooperation and the advancement of democracy and human rights.

16. The activities of the OSCE and of NATO are complementary and mutually reinforcing. NATO provides an important forum for political consultations among like-minded Allies as well as unique military capabilities to respond to security challenges. NATO's commitments to support, on a case-by-case basis and in accordance with Alliance procedures, peacekeeping activities under the responsibility of the OSCE and peacekeeping operations under the authority of the UN Security Council, will remain valid after enlargement. An enlarged Alliance would have greater capacity to support such peacekeeping activities and operations. OSCE discussions on a European security model for the 21st century should reflect the process of NATO enlargement but not delay it. A strengthened OSCE, an enlarged NATO, an active NACC and PfP would, together with other fora, form complementary parts of a broad, inclusive European security architecture, supporting the objective of an undivided Europe.

17. The Pact on Stability in Europe, which was entrusted to the OSCE and comprises numerous bilateral agreements and treaties between European countries, is a fundamental underpinning for security and stability in the whole of Europe. The Pact on Stability is aimed at developing good neighbourly relations, advancing respect for the human rights, including those of persons belonging to national minorities, and resolving disputes between European states. As noted in Chapter 1, the resolution of such disputes would be a factor in determining whether to invite a state to join the Alliance. Implementation of the Pact on Stability as well as of other international agreements already concluded can contribute to creating the conditions necessary for enlargement of NATO. In turn, enlargement of NATO's membership will also facilitate the implementation of existing agreements and full compliance with the obligations they contain.

18. Enlargement of the Alliance is aimed at extending stability in the Euro-Atlantic area and enhancing long-term security for all NATO member countries and others as well. The enlargement of NATO is a parallel

process with and will complement that of the European Union. Both NATO and the EU share common strategic interests as well as a broad approach to stability and security encompassing political, economic, social and environmental aspects, along with the defence dimension. Both enlargement processes will contribute significantly to extending security, stability and prosperity enjoyed by their members to other, like-minded, democratic European states. Through the conclusion of Euro-agreements, the EU has given a number of European states a perspective of eventual EU membership and integration into EU structures.

The enlargement of the two organizations will proceed autonomously according to their respective internal dynamics and processes. This means they are unlikely to proceed at precisely the same pace. But the Alliance views its own enlargement and that of the EU as mutually supportive and parallel processes which together will make a significant contribution to strengthening Europe's security structure. Thus, each organization should ensure that their respective processes are in fact mutually supportive of the goal of enhancing European stability and security. While no rigid parallelism is foreseen, each organization will need to consider developments in the other.

19. European Union members are committed to a Common Foreign and Security Policy which shall include all questions related to the security of the Union, including the eventual framing of a common defence policy, which might in time lead to a common defence compatible with that of the Atlantic Alliance. The WEU is an integral part of the development of the Union. In its dual role as defence component of the EU and European pillar of the Atlantic Alliance, the WEU brings an important additional dimension to European security. Acknowledging this dual role, and wishing to contribute to its further development, NATO Heads of State and Government, in January 1994, expressed their readiness to make collective assets of the Alliance available, on the basis of consultations in the North Atlantic Council, for WEU operations undertaken by the European Allies in pursuit of their Common Foreign and Security Policy.

20. All full members of the WEU are also members of NATO. Because of the cumulative effect of the security safeguards of Article V of the modified Brussels Treaty and of Article 5 of the Washington Treaty, the maintenance of this linkage is essential. Both enlargement processes should, therefore, be compatible and mutually supportive. At the same time, the WEU is being developed as the defence component of the European Union, which strengthens the relationship between the two

organisations. An eventual broad congruence of European membership in NATO, EU and WEU would have positive effects on European security. The Alliance should at an appropriate time give particular consideration to countries with a perspective of EU membership, and which have shown an interest in joining NATO, in order to consider, on the basis indicated in this study, how they can contribute to transatlantic security within the Washington Treaty and to determine whether to invite them to join NATO.

21. All CFE States Parties acknowledge the Treaty's continued fundamental role in building and maintaining European stability and security. This is also shared by all other OSCE participating states. NATO Allies consider the CFE Treaty as the cornerstone of European security. Therefore, it is of fundamental importance to preserve the Treaty's integrity and to ensure its full and timely implementation. NATO as such is not a signatory of the CFE Treaty, nor of any other arms control agreement. Therefore, from a legal point of view, NATO's enlargement per se has no impact on the Treaty. In any case, possible implications of NATO's enlargement for the CFE Treaty can only be assessed when the actual enlargement is taking place. Since there is no decision as yet on the timing and the scope of NATO's enlargement, it would be premature to draw any conclusions at this stage.

22. The existing confidence-building, disarmament and arms control agreements are fundamental underpinnings for security and stability in the whole of Europe. NATO must contribute to their continuing validity and relevance in the course of its enlargement process. Enlargement could strengthen the Alliance's ability to promote further arms control and disarmament measures and ways to control proliferation of WMD.

C. Relations with Russia

23. Russia has an important contribution to make to European stability and security. We have agreed that constructive, cooperative relations of mutual respect, benefit and friendship between the Alliance and Russia are a key element for security and stability in Europe. In June 1994, we agreed that such relations should be developed in a way that reflects common objectives and complements and reinforces relations with all other states, is transparent and is not directed against the interests of third countries. Cooperative NATO-Russia relations are in the interest not only of NATO and Russia, but of all other states in the OSCE area.

24. NATO and Russia have agreed to pursue a broad, enhanced dialogue and cooperation in areas where Russia has unique and important contributions

to make, commensurate with its weight and responsibility as a major European, international and nuclear power.

25. In June 1994, NATO and Russia agreed to set in train the development of a far-reaching, cooperative NATO-Russia relationship aimed at enhancing mutual confidence and openness. At that time Russia signed the PfP Framework Document. By December, agreement had been reached on Russia's Individual Partnership Programme and areas for pursuance of a broad, enhanced NATO-Russia dialogue and cooperation beyond PfP, which were formally accepted by Russia on 31 May 1995.

26. The Alliance considers that it is desirable to develop the NATO-Russia relationship even further as part of our broad approach to developing a cooperative security architecture in Europe. NATO and Russia have initiated a dialogue, to be pursued in our newly established relationship beyond the PfP, on the future direction our relationship should take, with the aim of achieving by the end of this year a political framework for NATO-Russia relations elaborating basic principles for security cooperation as well as for the development of mutual political consultations. A stronger NATO-Russia relationship should form another cornerstone of a new, inclusive and comprehensive security structure in Europe. NATO-Russia cooperation can help to overcome any lingering distrust from the Cold War period, and help ensure that Europe is never again divided into opposing camps. This further development of the NATO-Russia relationship, and its possible eventual formalization, should take place in rough parallel with NATO's own enlargement, with the goal of further strengthening stability and security in Europe. The substance and form of this enhanced relationship will be developed through a NATO-Russia dialogue.

27. NATO-Russia relations should reflect Russia's significance in European security and be based on reciprocity, mutual respect and confidence, no *"surprise"* decisions by either side which could affect the interests of the other. This relationship can only flourish if it is rooted in strict compliance with international commitments and obligations, such as those under the UN Charter, the OSCE, including the Code of Conduct and the CFE Treaty, and full respect for the sovereignty of other independent states. NATO decisions, however, cannot be subject to any veto or droit de regard by a non-member state, nor can the Alliance be subordinated to another European security institution.

28. Russia has raised concerns with respect to the enlargement process of the Alliance. The Alliance is addressing these concerns in developing its wider relationship with Russia and the Alliance has made it clear that the

enlargement process including the associated military arrangements will threaten no-one and contribute to a developing broad European security architecture based on true cooperation throughout the whole of Europe, enhancing security and stability for all.

D. Effects of the decision-making process on European security and stability

29. The decision-making process on enlargement will be in accordance with the Washington Treaty. Each invitation will be decided on its own merits, case by case, and in accordance with the principles identified in this study, taking into account political and security related developments in the whole of Europe. It will be important, particularly in the meantime, not to foreclose the possibility of eventual Alliance membership for any European state in accordance with Article 10 of the Washington Treaty.

30. Countries could be invited to join sequentially or several countries could be simultaneously invited to join, bearing in mind that all Allies will decide by consensus on each invitation, i.e. new Allies must join consensus for subsequent invitations. There could be two or more sets of simultaneous invitations. Sequential accession could reduce the implication that others might be excluded and make it easier to begin with one or more countries but could also risk extending the calendar of accessions and thereby diverting attention from other important Alliance business. Simultaneous accessions would avoid the possibility of veto by new members on others joining at the same time; any decision on simultaneous accession should take into account relations among the prospective new members concerned and the impact on other states, including their relationship with NATO. Legislative/ratification considerations in Allied countries related to the accession of new member(s) to the Washington Treaty should also be taken into account.

Concerns have already been expressed in the context of the discussion of the enlargement of NATO that a new member might *"close the door"* behind it to new admissions in the future of other countries which may also aspire to NATO membership. Such a situation must be avoided; the Alliance rests upon commonality of views and a commitment to work for consensus; part of the evaluation of the qualifications of a possible new member will be its demonstrated commitment to that process and those values. We will invite prospective new members to confirm that they understand and accept this and act in good faith accordingly. The Alliance may require, if appropriate, specific political commitments in the course of accession negotiations.

Chapter 3: *How NACC and PfP can contribute concretely to the enlargement process*

A. Introduction

31. The PfP and NACC can help to ensure that, in accepting new members, the Alliance will contribute to enhanced security and stability in an undivided Europe, fundamental goals of the Alliance, as discussed in Chapter II. As the enlargement process proceeds, NACC/PfP will continue to provide the fundamental framework for developing relations with partner countries. Dynamic NACC/PfP cooperation is an integral part of the European security architecture, deepening interaction and extending security and stability throughout Europe, and as a means to strengthen relations with partner countries, whether possible new members or not. In the context of enlargement, this will require particular attention and effort by the Alliance.

32. PfP will play an important role both to help prepare possible new members, through their participation in PfP activities, for the benefits and responsibilities of eventual membership and as a means to strengthen relations with partner countries which may be unlikely to join the Alliance early or at all. There will be a need to ensure that appropriate human and financial resources are directed to support those activities in accordance with PfP funding policy.

33. NACC will continue, as it has since its inception in 1991, to play a significant role in building confidence and drawing NATO Allies and cooperation partners closer together. In the context of enlargement, the importance of NACC will be enhanced, in particular, as a common forum encompassing NATO Allies and NACC/PfP partners for dialogue and consultation on political and security-related issues and for cooperation among its members to strengthen security.

B. The Continuing Role of the NACC and the PfP in Strengthening European Security

34. The Partnership for Peace is a key element in NATO's political and military cooperation programmes with non-member OSCE countries which deepens interaction, cooperation and stability in Europe and contributes to the overall goal of transparency. PfP is only at the beginning of its development; its full potential has not yet been achieved; and its continuing importance will not be affected by enlargement.

35. Within the broader PfP framework, a critical aspect is that partners reaffirmed their commitment to the principles of the UN and the OSCE and their readiness to develop cooperative military relations with NATO

to strengthen their ability to undertake peacekeeping and other missions under the authority of the UN and/or the responsibility of the OSCE. The Alliance should ensure that PfP gets all due attention and credit in this regard.

36. For countries that do not become members, NACC/PfP must constitute: a continuing vehicle for active cooperation with NATO; concrete evidence of NATO's continuing support and concern for their security; and their primary link to the Alliance, as a key Euro-Atlantic security institution, including for consultation with NATO in the event an active partner perceives a direct threat to its territorial integrity, political independence or security. The Alliance will maintain the importance, vitality and credibility of NACC/PfP as enlargement evolves to retain their value for countries which may be unlikely to join the Alliance early or at all. Maintaining the vitality of NACC/PfP may require new approaches and mechanisms to be devised in parallel to the Alliance's enlargement process. In this context, Ministers have instructed the Council to explore the scope for integrating the existing cooperative structures and procedures for NACC and the Partnership for Peace.

37. PfP cooperation should be further developed in order to:
    • help partners to further develop democratic control of their armed forces and transparency in defence planning and budgeting processes, although this will largely depend on these countries' own efforts;
    • enhance the network of military and defence-related cooperation to provide effective support to partners in adapting their defence arrangements to the new security environment;
    • develop the cooperative features of PfP, e.g., through enhancing partners' involvement in developing, planning and implementing PfP activities, in particular by increasing their capability/readiness to contribute with others to peacekeeping, humanitarian, search and rescue and other activities to be agreed;
    • strengthen the confidence-building and transparent character of defence-related and military cooperation, both with Allies and among partners;
    • complement the development of interoperable forces by adequate mechanisms to duly involve partners in planning and carrying out joint peacekeeping operations.

C. The Role of PfP in Preparing for Membership

38. PfP activities and programmes are open to all partners, who themselves decide which opportunities to pursue and how intensively to work with the Alliance through the Partnership. This varying degree of participation is a key element of the self-differentiation process. Active participation in PfP will play an important role in possible new members' preparation to join the Alliance, although it will not guarantee Alliance membership. Active participation in NACC/PfP will provide the framework for possible new members to establish patterns of political and military cooperation with the Alliance to facilitate a transition to membership. Through PfP planning, joint exercises and other PfP activities, including seminars, workshops and day-to-day representation in Brussels and at Mons, possible new members will increasingly become acquainted with the functioning of the Alliance, including with respect to policy-making, peacekeeping and crisis management. Possible new members' commitment to the shared principles and values of the Alliance will be indicated by their international behaviour and adherence to relevant OSCE commitments; however, their participation in PfP will provide a further important means to demonstrate such commitment as well as their ability to contribute to common defence.

39. For possible new members, PfP will contribute to their preparation both politically and militarily, to familiarise them with Alliance structures and procedures and to deepen their understanding of the obligations and rights that membership will entail.

    PfP will help partners undertake necessary defence management reforms as they establish the processes and mechanisms necessary to run a democratically controlled military organisation, in areas such as transparent national defence planning, resource allocation and budgeting, appropriate legislation and parliamentary and public accountability. PfP will assist possible new members to develop well-established democratic accountability and practices and to demonstrate their commitment to internationally-accepted norms of behaviour. Within the scope of the Framework Document, PfP also provides a means to promote and develop interoperability with Alliance forces by familiarising possible new members with important elements for interoperability.

40. The PfP Planning and Review Process and PfP exercises will introduce partners to collective defence planning and pave the way for more detailed operational planning. A biennial PfP Planning and Review Process has been offered to all Partners on an optional basis and provides a means of self-differentiation. Participation in the process will be the

most effective way to develop, in the longer term, Partner forces that are better able to operate with those of the NATO Allies. Cooperation between Partners and the Alliance in the process will be broadened and deepened over time as appropriate. Results of this process should be incorporated in Partner defence plans and reflected in PfP, IPPs and the Partnership Work Programme as appropriate. While new members will not be required to achieve full interoperability with NATO before joining the Alliance, they will need to meet certain minimum standards essential to a functioning and credible Alliance. These standards will continue to be developed by NATO and will be based in part on conclusions reached through the Planning and Review Process. Partners' own efforts will largely determine how quickly they progress in preparing for possible NATO membership, although outside assistance may facilitate progress.

41. The preparation of possible new members interested in joining NATO can be facilitated by an appropriate reinforcement and deepening of their Individual Partnership Programmes. Such a reinforcement and deepening is a key to self-differentiation. Among other things, it would allow partners to distinguish themselves by demonstrating their capabilities and their commitment with a view to possible NATO membership and to contribute to Alliance missions. Concerning the process of preparing for membership, the premature development of measures outside PfP for possible new members should be avoided. A clear distinction should be maintained between participation in PfP and an eventual invitation to join the Alliance. There will come a point, after a country has been invited to join the Alliance, when specific measures for preparing the accession of that country will have to be devised.

Chapter 4: *How to ensure that enlargement strengthens the effectiveness of the Alliance, preserves its ability to perform its core functions of common defence as well as to undertake peacekeeping and other new missions, and upholds the principles and objectives of the Washington Treaty*

A. Maintaining the Effectiveness of the Alliance to Perform its Core Functions and New Missions

42. In enlarging its membership, the Alliance will want to ensure that it maintains its ability to take important decisions quickly on the basis of consensus and that enlargement results in an Alliance fully able to carry out both its core functions and its new missions. In addition to being fundamentally important in its own right, the Alliance's ability to act

quickly, decisively and effectively is crucial to its role in the European security architecture and to its ability to integrate new members into it.

43. On joining the Alliance, new members must accept the full obligations of the Washington Treaty. This includes participation in the consultation process within the Alliance and the principle of decision-making by consensus, which requires a commitment to build consensus within the Alliance on all issues of concern to it. New members must also be prepared to contribute to collective defence under Article 5, to the Alliance's new evolving missions and to Alliance budgets. This may include appropriate contributions to the Alliance's military force and command structures and infrastructure. New members must accept and conform with the principles, policies and procedures adopted by all members of the Alliance at the time that new members join. In this respect, new members deciding to participate in the integrated military structure must accept the applicable policies and procedures.

44. NATO must ensure that all Alliance military obligations, particularly those under Article 5, will be met in an enlarged Alliance. This will require a case-by-case assessment of the military factors, including preparation time for NATO to take on new Article 5 commitments, for each prospective new member, taking into account the strategic environment, possible risks faced by potential new members, the capabilities and interoperability of their forces, their approach and that of the allies to the stationing of foreign forces on their territory, and the relevant reinforcement capabilities of Alliance forces, including strategic mobility. The Alliance will also have to ensure the accessibility of its forces to new members' territory for reinforcement, exercises, crisis management and, if applicable, stationing. This issue will need to be considered in the context of deciding individual new members' accession.

45. The Alliance will have to take a number of elements into account to ensure that NATO maintains its military credibility when it enlarges. Many of these elements may require further analysis and development by the Alliance in the course of the enlargement process. The Alliance bears the responsibility for determining the measures taken to maintain military credibility within each of these elements. These elements, which are developed further in later sections of this chapter and in chapter 5, fall into the following categories:

Collective Defence

A key principle of the enlargement process is that new members will be expected not only to benefit from, but also to contribute to, the

Alliance's collective defence. They should also be prepared to contribute to other Alliance missions;

Command Structure

All new members should participate in an appropriate way in the command structure of the Alliance. New members joining the integrated structure will need to be integrated into existing NATO headquarters. The Alliance will have to consider whether a limited number of new headquarters may be needed and any need for existing headquarters to cover new Areas of Responsibility. NATO operations will be controlled by existing or new NATO headquarters or, as appropriate, future CJTF headquarters;

Conventional Forces

Training and Exercises New members will need to participate in NATO exercises, including those designed to ensure the common defence. Exercises should be held regularly on new members' territory;

Nuclear Forces

The supreme guarantee of the security of the Allies is provided by the strategic nuclear forces of the Alliance. New members will share the benefits and responsibilities from this in the same way as all other Allies in accordance with the Strategic Concept. New members will be expected to support the concept of deterrence and the essential role nuclear weapons play in the Alliance's strategy of war prevention as set forth in the Strategic Concept;

Force Structure

It is important for NATO's force structure that other Allies' forces can be deployed, when and if appropriate, on the territory of new members. The Alliance has no a priori requirement for the stationing of Alliance troops on the territory of new members. New members should participate in the Alliance's force structure. How this will be achieved may require additional considerations to include: whether new members should develop specially-trained units capable of reinforcing NATO forces and of being reinforced by NATO units; the prepositioning of materiel in critical areas; how to ensure that infrastructure is adequate to meet planned missions; and whether there is a need to increase strategic and intra-theatre mobility;

Intelligence

New members will have the opportunity to participate to the fullest extent possible in the NATO intelligence processes;

Finance

New members will be expected to contribute their share to NATO's commonly funded programmes. They should also be aware that they face substantial financial obligations when joining the Alliance;

Interoperability

All new members will be expected to make every effort to meet NATO interoperability standards, in particular for command, control and communication equipment. New members will have to incorporate NATO standard operational procedures in selected areas, including for their national headquarters.

46. A smooth and effective decision-making process in an enlarged Alliance will be key to preserving its effectiveness. Maintenance of the consensus principle will be essential in the political, military and defence areas. All Allies must therefore be willing to work constructively towards this. To this end, it will be important that prospective new members become familiar with the Alliance decision-making process, and the modalities and traditions of consensus and compromise, before joining. The highest priority should be given to a new member's involvement in the appropriate elements of the decision-making processes and military commands.

B. The Military and Defence Implications of Enlargement
(I) Collective Defence

47. As stated in paragraph 38 of the Strategic Concept, *"the collective nature of Alliance defence is embodied in practical arrangements that enable the Allies to enjoy the crucial political, military and resource advantages of collective defence, and prevent the renationalisation of defence policies, without depriving the Allies of their sovereignty. These arrangements are based on an integrated military structure as well as on cooperation and coordination agreements. Key features include collective force planning; common operational planning; multinational formations; the stationing of forces outside home territory, where appropriate on a mutual basis; crisis management and reinforcement arrangements; procedures for consultation; common standards and procedures of equipment, training and logistics; joint and combined exercises; and infrastructure, armaments and logistics cooperation".*

48. There are currently three forms under which Allies contribute to NATO collective defence: full participation in the integrated military structure

and the collective defence planning process; non-membership of the integrated military structure but full participation in the collective defence planning process together with a series of coordination agreements providing for cooperation with the integrated military structure in certain defined areas; and non-participation in the integrated military structure and collective defence planning but cooperation with the integrated military structure in more limited defined areas under agreements between the Chief of Defence and the Major NATO Commanders (MNCs). As a general principle, we should avoid new forms of contribution to NATO collective defence which would complicate unnecessarily practical cooperation among Allies and the Alliance's decision-making process.

49. Against the background of existing arrangements for contributing to collective defence, Allies will want to know how possible new members intend to contribute to NATO's collective defence and will explore all aspects of this question in detail through bilateral dialogue prior to accession negotiations. In this context, the ability to contribute and the manner in which a possible new member intends to contribute to collective defence will be important criteria for Allies in deciding whether such a potential new member is capable and willing to contribute to security and stability in the trans-Atlantic area within the meaning of Article 10 of the Washington Treaty.

50. The Alliance will adopt a flexible approach to assimilating new members into its defence and military structures and its planning processes. The approach taken will ensure that an enlarged NATO maintains a credible military posture.

(ii) Command Structure

51. NATO's command structure must be prepared for the probability that new members will want to join the integrated military structure. If enlargement takes place consecutively, considerable military flexibility will be required with regard to the establishment of new areas of responsibility and the related command structure. A broad plan will therefore be needed to ensure the maximum effectiveness and flexibility of the command structure following the accession of new members, bearing in mind the potential effect of the CJTF concept and of any structural adjustments.

52. NATO headquarters may be required on the territory of new members to cover the revised tasks and AORs resulting from their accession. Although it may be possible to upgrade new members' existing headquarters if necessary to meet an as yet undefined NATO requirement, existing command, control and communications equipment and infrastructure is

unlikely to meet minimum NATO standards. The establishment of head-quarters on the territory of new members may also have implications for NATO's existing command structure. The building of new headquarters and/or the upgrading of existing headquarters to NATO standards would involve significant costs although progress on the development of the CJTF concept may have a bearing on Alliance headquarters requirements. A country-specific review of the requirements and costs should be under-taken prior to a new member joining the integrated military structure.

53. Multinationality remains a key feature of Alliance policy. Any new NATO headquarters on the territory of a new member would therefore require multinational representation; this should reflect operational needs. New members will also have to be represented as appropriate at major head-quarters (MSC and above), support elements, commonly-funded NATO Agencies, and on the International Military Staff. Enlargement would therefore probably require a review of the size of staffs at most NATO headquarters and national representation. This process would inevitably be complicated if new members join consecutively.

(iii) Conventional Forces-Training and Exercises

54. The presence of Allied Forces on the territory of other members con-tributes to strengthening the Alliance's ability to perform its fundamen-tal security tasks, fostering Alliance cohesion and expressing solidarity and confidence. This presence could take various forms. The stationing of Allied forces offers specific military advantages in relation to collective defence. It allows a threat or an attack to be countered earlier, and pro-vides more time to prepare and deploy reinforcements, enabling the most effective use to be made of mobility. Moreover, military forces operate more effectively when they are familiar with the terrain and con-ditions. However, the redeployment of existing Allied forces from their current locations or the prepositioning of equipment would be expen-sive. There also is a risk that it could give a misleading impression of Alliance concerns. The regular and frequent presence of Allied forces on exercise or when other situations demand is another way to demonstrate NATO's commitment to collective defence. This option may not be ade-quate in all cases. It would in any event require effective rapid reaction and reinforcement capabilities and planning, and adequate warning time to allow for political decision making and the deployment of forces in time of crisis. Other options might include dual basing of air assets, or the prepositioning of equipment and ammunition (e.g., increased prepo-sitioned materiel in key areas and increased storage sites for such materiel in key geographical areas).

55. Individual Allies' policy on the stationing of other Allies' forces on their territory in peacetime varies considerably, taking into account a range of national and broader factors. For new members, the peacetime stationing of other Allies' forces on their territory should neither be a condition of membership nor foreclosed as an option. Decisions on the stationing of Allies' conventional forces on the territory of new members will have to be taken by the Alliance in the light of the benefits both to the Alliance as a whole and to particular new members, the military advantages of such a presence, the Alliance's military capacity for rapid and effective reinforcement, the views of the new members concerned, the cost of possible military options, and the wider political and strategic impact. All Allies must of course be prepared in times of crisis or war to allow other Allies' forces to enter and operate on their territory, and to provide essential host nation support as mutually agreed, to enable NATO to provide effective common defence.

56. Individual Allies' policy on stationing their forces outside their borders in peacetime also varies considerably. Some Allies are, for example, legally constrained from doing so. For new members the peacetime stationing of forces on other Allies' territory should neither be a condition of membership nor foreclosed as an option. All Allies are, however, prepared in principle to deploy their forces outside their territory in the Treaty area as part of their contribution to NATO collective defence, taking into account factors such as operational capabilities and geographic limitations. New members should be expected to be similarly prepared.

57. Multinational training and exercises on the territory of new members will contribute significantly to maintaining Alliance military capability and effectiveness and enhance the ability of the Alliance to fulfil its full range of missions.

Such exercising and training would help familiarise the forces involved with the terrain and operating conditions, and would contribute directly to supporting Article 5 commitments. Reinforcement should also be exercised from time to time. The terms on which such activities currently take place vary between Allies and have to take account of national factors. However, as a general principle, new members should be ready to host multinational training and exercises relating to all Alliance missions.

(iv) Nuclear Forces

58. The coverage provided by Article 5, including its nuclear component, will apply to new members. There is no a priori requirement for the stationing of nuclear weapons on the territory of new members. In light of

both the current international environment and the potential threats facing the Alliance, NATO's current nuclear posture will, for the foreseeable future, continue to meet the requirements of an enlarged Alliance. There is, therefore, no need now to change or modify any aspect of NATO's nuclear posture or policy, but the longer term implications of enlargement for both will continue to be evaluated. NATO should retain its existing nuclear capabilities along with its right to modify its nuclear posture as circumstances warrant. New members will, as do current members, contribute to the development and implementation of NATO's strategy, including its nuclear components; new members should be eligible to join the Nuclear Planning Group and its subordinate bodies and to participate in nuclear consultation during exercises and crisis. Decisions on the modalities and specifics of this contribution will be based on consultations, and agreements among Allies.

(v) Force Structures

59. The Alliance's military strength and cohesion depends on its multinational forces and structures, and the fair sharing of risks, responsibilities, costs and benefits. Current force structures are based primarily on the requirements of collective defence, but Alliance involvement in non-Article 5 operations will continue to influence future capabilities. All Alliance nations have a high degree of ability to operate together, although there is room for further improvement.

60. Subject to any changes in the security environment, the main characteristics of current NATO force structures will remain valid in an enlarged Alliance. However, the Alliance will need to pay special attention to the requirements of inter-regional reinforcement, and their potential impact on the various force categories. To ensure continued Alliance military effectiveness, current and prospective new members must be committed to developing, manning and supporting NATO's new force structures. New members' forces would be expected to take part in the full spectrum of Alliance missions to the extent appropriate to their capabilities, and taking into account the need for case by case consideration of non-Article 5 missions. The further development of Alliance military structures, including force levels and readiness, should facilitate such involvement across the spectrum of potential Alliance missions.

61. Multinational forces have an increased political and military importance. Thus the increasing need for mobility, flexibility and inter-service and multinational interoperability in undertaking both defence and new missions means that current Alliance policy on multinationality should

apply when new members' forces join NATO force structure, consistent with the need to maintain military effectiveness.

62. There is a continuing need to address current limitations in reaction force capabilities, which have to be taken into account to ensure that there is no reduction in military effectiveness. The principle of multinationality should also apply in integrating new members' forces into main defence forces. No change of current policy towards augmentation forces would seem to be necessary as a result of enlargement. There will, however, be a substantial impact, the extent of which has yet to be determined, on contingency and reinforcement planning including force requirements and host nation support arrangements. Prepositioning of equipment, and both intra-theatre and inter-theatre lift, can contribute to flexibility and military effectiveness. Further examination of these elements will be required when enlargement occurs.

(vi) Intelligence Sharing

63. Sharing of intelligence among Allies contributes to the effectiveness of the Alliance. New members will bring to the Alliance both increased requirements and capabilities in the intelligence field. Intelligence sharing is based on mutual trust and co-operation. New members must be able tosafeguard NATO information according to Alliance standards.

C. Security Investment Programme (SIP)

64. The NATO Security Investment Programme should be used to accelerate the assimilation process of new members. The scope of this will depend upon the terms under which new members will participate. Procedurally and organisationally, the incorporation of new members into the Programme will not present problems although the process may take time. The renewed prioritisation and resource allocation mechanisms are well suited to deal with new requirements resulting from enlargement.

65. Financially, new members would be expected to contribute their share, as from the start, to all new programme activities, with a contribution level based, in a general way, on *"ability to pay"*. Because of the time needed in an investment programme to bring activities to implementation, and because of the limited absorption capacity of new members, financial implications will be limited in the early years. Enlarged participation in the programme should therefore be possible without impact on the implementation of existing commitments and programmes. It is important, however, to get prospective new members involved in the

planning and preparatory processes as soon as possible and to ensure that they are fully aware of their prospective liabilities.

D. Administration and Budgets

66. Without knowing the number of prospective new members it is only possible to address management issues in a general manner. Enlargement will lead to new activities and a need for increased resources. Additional office space will be needed at NATO HQ to accommodate new members and possible increases to the staffs of the IS and IMS. Operating and capital costs in the Civil Budget will grow. New members will be expected to contribute. Cost shares must be calculated and decisions taken concerning their obligations. Enlargement will also mean increases in the Military Budget, but the actual budgetary consequences will depend in large part on the new members' level of participation.

67. It will be important to ensure that potential new members are fully aware that they face considerable financial obligations when joining the Alliance.

Chapter 5: *What are the implications of membership for new members, including their rights and obligations, and what do they need to do to prepare for membership?*

68. New members will be full members of the Alliance, enjoying all the rights and assuming all the obligations under the Washington Treaty. There must be no "second tier" security guarantees or members within the Alliance and no modifications of the Washington Treaty for those who join. Possible new members should prepare themselves on this basis. Although this Chapter describes the principal rights and obligations of new member states, some more specific rights and obligations are covered elsewhere, in Chapters 2, 3 and 4.

A. What will be Expected Politically of New Members

69. Commitments entered into by new member states should be the same as for present Allies, including acceptance of the principles, policies and procedures already adopted by all members of the Alliance at the time that new members join. Willingness and ability to meet such commitments, not only on paper but in practice, would be a critical factor in any decision to invite a country to join.

70. Bearing in mind that there is no fixed or rigid list of criteria for inviting new members to join the Alliance, possible new member states will, nevertheless, be expected to:

- Conform to basic principles embodied in the Washington Treaty: democracy, individual liberty and the rule of law;
- Accept NATO as a community of like-minded nations joined together for collective defence and the preservation of peace and security, with each nation contributing to the security and defence from which all member nations benefit;
- Be firmly committed to principles, objectives and undertakings included in the Partnership for Peace Framework Document;
- Commit themselves to good faith efforts to build consensus within the Alliance on all issues, since consensus is the basis of Alliance cohesion and decision-making;
- Undertake to participate fully in the Alliance consultation and decision-making process on political and security issues of concern to the Alliance;
- Establish a permanent representation at NATO HQ;
- Establish an appropriate national military representation at SHAPE/SACLANT;
- Be prepared to nominate qualified candidates to serve on the International Staff and in NATO agencies;
- Provide qualified personnel to serve on the International Military Staff and in the Integrated Military Structure if and as appropriate;
- Contribute to Alliance budgets, based on budget shares to be agreed;
- Participate, as appropriate, in the exchange of Allied intelligence, which is based entirely on national contributions;
- Apply NATO security rules and procedures;
- Accept the Documents which provide the basis for the existing policies of the Alliance. ([1])

71. The Alliance expects new members not to *"close the door"* to the accession of one or more later candidate members, as referred to also in paragraph 30 of Chapter 2.

B. What Prospective New Members will need to do Politically to Prepare Themselves for Membership

72. Prospective members will have to have:
- Demonstrated a commitment to and respect for OSCE norms and principles, including the resolution of ethnic disputes, external territorial disputes including irredentist claims or internal jurisdictional disputes by peaceful means, as referred to also in paragraph 6 of Chapter 1;
- Shown a commitment to promoting stability and well-being by economic liberty, social justice and environmental responsibility;

- Established appropriate democratic and civilian control of their defence force;
- Undertaken a commitment to ensure that adequate resources are devoted to achieving the obligations described in section A and C.

C. What Will Be Expected Militarily of New Members

73. New members of the Alliance must be prepared to share the roles, risks, responsibilities, benefits, and burdens of common security and collective defence. They should be expected to subscribe to Alliance strategy as set out in the Strategic Concept and refined in subsequent Ministerial statements.

74. An important element in new members' military contribution will be a commitment in good faith to pursue the objectives of standardization which are essential to Alliance strategy and operational effectiveness. New members should concentrate, in the first instance, on interoperability. As a minimum, they should accept NATO doctrine and policies relating to standardization and in addition aim at achieving a sufficient level of training and equipment to operate effectively with NATO forces. PfP cooperation, including the Planning and Review Process, can help to improve the interoperability of Partners' forces with those of NATO Allies and aspiring new members should be expected to participate actively in PfP activities; but these are limited in scope to forces made available by Partners for cooperation in peacekeeping, humanitarian and SAR missions, and related training and exercises.

D. What Prospective New Members Will Need to do Militarily to Prepare Themselves for Membership

75. The ability of prospective members to contribute militarily to collective defence and to the Alliance's new missions will be a factor in deciding whether to invite them to join the Alliance.

76. New members will need to adapt themselves to the fact that NATO's strategy and force structure are designed to exploit multinationality and flexibility to provide effective defence at minimum cost. NATO policy is therefore heavily dependent on standardization, particularly in the areas of operations, administration and material. Current NATO standardization priorities include commonality of doctrines and procedures, interoperability of command, control and communications and major weapon systems, and interchangeability of ammunition and primary combat supplies.

77. There are at present over 1200 agreements and publications that new members should undertake to comply with. Compliance should be an evolutionary and controlled process to enhance Alliance operational effectiveness. Although national participation in standardization is optional,

there are a number of areas, such as communication and information systems and measures to facilitate reinforcements where military necessity requires participation. One way of achieving improved interoperability might be for new members to select units that can act as cornerstone units around which the rest of their forces can be developed with priority being given to maximizing these units' interoperability with existing NATO units. To determine the minimum requirements necessary for operational effectiveness, a review of the STANAGs and Allied Publications is already under way. A country-by-country assessment of prospective new members' standardization will also be required, based on levels of standardization displayed during the full range of PfP military and defence activities. A proposal should be developed by the Alliance in consultation with the prospective new member so that it will understand what will be expected of it. In addition, NATO schools and training will need to be developed so that the forces of new members can achieve interoperability with NATO in a reasonable time, and new members can adapt to NATO doctrine across a broad spectrum of activities.

78. Although the funding of new members' enhanced interoperability is their responsibility, it poses important challenges for the Alliance as a whole. There is a military imperative to achieve the minimum level of interoperability required for military effectiveness as quickly as possible. There is also a political imperative to demonstrate intra-Alliance cohesion, to ensure that new members feel that they are participating fully in the Alliance and to enable them to make an equitable contribution to collective defence at an early stage. In principle, both objectives should be achieved within the existing arrangements for funding Allies' development, procurement, infrastructure and other costs (i.e. using national resources and the Security Investment Programme as appropriate).

Footnote:

1. These include, in particular:
   - The Agreement on the Status of the North Atlantic Treaty Organization, National Representatives and International Staff (Ottawa Convention, 1951);
   - The NATO Agreement on the Mutual Safeguarding of Secrecy of Inventions relating to Defence, and for which applications for Patents have been made (Paris, 1960);
   - The Agreement between the Parties to the North Atlantic Treaty regarding the Status on their Forces (London, 1951);

- The NATO Agreement on the Communication of Technical Information for defence Purposes Brussels, 1970);

as well as

- The Strategic Concept;
- Summit Declarations and NAC decisions in Ministerial and permanent session as reflect in NAC Communiques, including those issued in Oslo in June 1992 and Brussels in December 1992 in which the Alliance undertook to support, on a case-by-case basis in accordance with its own procedures, peacekeeping activities under the responsibility of the OSCE and peacekeeping operations under the authority of the UN Security Council, including by making available Alliance resources and expertise;
- Documents on cooperation between NATO and any partner state already agreed with new member(s) join the Alliance,

recognizing that Alliance polices evolve over time and in the light of new circumstances.

Chapter 6: *Modalities according to which the enlargement process should proceed*

79. The modalities for enlargement flow from Article 10 of the Washington Treaty. Previous accessions in accordance with Article 10 need not be considered precise models for future accessions, since the general political and security context of future accessions will be different as well as the number, individual circumstances and characteristics of new acceding members. In this context, a process which is predictable and transparent with respect to new accessions may be required to provide reassurance to public and legislative opinion in existing member states. The modalities for future accession should avoid any suggestion of different classes of membership.

80. While each invitation to join the Alliance will be decided on its own merits, case by case, the timing of future accessions could be sequential or in one or more simultaneous sets. In any case, it will be important to make clear that the Alliance remains open to further accessions by countries not among the earliest to be invited to join. A declaration at the time of the first invitation(s) being issued which clearly stated this would both reassure those countries that would not be among the first to be invited and reduce the likelihood of some of those countries submitting unsolicited applications to join the Alliance.

81. The precise timing, sequence and content of the accession process need to be considered carefully, particularly with respect to talks and negotiations with countries to be invited to join. Detailed briefings to provide necessary information to such countries will be needed at an early stage of the accession process, prior to formal negotiations. The NAC will decide on beginning any necessary exploratory contacts, after which the following steps would be required for any future accession to the Washington Treaty:
    - a decision by the NAC (at an appropriate level) to authorize the Secretary General to inform a country/countries that the Allies are favourably disposed to its/their accession, and to enter into talks with it/them;
    - a formal notification from the country/countries to the Secretary General of its/their firm commitment, in accordance with domestic legal requirements, to join the Alliance;
    - detailed consultations with the country/countries concerned about the protocol of accession;
    - formulation by the Allies of the protocol of accession;
    - approval and signature of the accession protocol by the NAC;
    - ratification, acceptance or approval of the accession protocol by the Allies and entry into force;
    - formal invitation to the country/countries to accede to the North Atlantic Treaty;
    - deposition by the country/countries of its/their instrument(s) of accession with the U.S. Government.
    It may not be feasible for countries invited to join to provide assurances that all domestic requirements for it/them to do so have been met together with formal notification of its/their desire to join. Precision may therefore be required on this point. It will be important, however, to avoid legislative ratification procedures for new accessions going forward in existing Allied countries without assurance that the country concerned wants to and will accede.
82. It will need to be decided to what extent preparations for membership by countries can be undertaken before formal accession or whether many of these can be left until after formal accession. When to deal with budgetary and administrative issues will need to be decided. Consultations regarding accession with any country concerned should not delay those with any other, i.e. the pace of movement towards accession by a number of invited countries should not be dictated by that of the slowest.

Final Communiqué of the Ministerial Meeting of the North Atlantic Council in Sintra, Portugal—29 May 1997

1. We have met in Sintra today to carry forward the Alliance's ongoing process of internal and external adaptation, and to prepare the major decisions our Heads of State and Government will take at their Summit meeting on 8th-9th July in Madrid. This Summit will shape the new NATO as a foundation for the development of a truly cooperative European security structure as we move towards the 21st century. Allied solidarity and cohesion as reflected in the core functions, including our common commitment to collective defence, and a strong transatlantic partnership will remain the backbone of the Alliance's success in this endeavour.

2. We are determined to raise to a qualitatively new level our political and military cooperation with our Partners, building upon the success of the North Atlantic Cooperation Council (NACC) and the Partnership for Peace (PfP). We have therefore decided to propose to our Partners to launch together at tomorrow's NACC meeting the Euro-Atlantic Partnership Council (EAPC), the framework of which we have developed with Partners over the last months. During the past five years, the NACC has served as a key forum for bringing Europe together. The EAPC, in replacing the NACC, will unite the positive experience of NACC and PfP by providing the overarching framework for political and security-related consultations and for enhanced cooperation under PfP, whose basic elements will remain valid. We are looking forward to tomorrow's first meeting with our Partners in the EAPC.

   We are pleased with the dynamic and successful development of the Partnership for Peace with 27 countries. The Partnership has brought us closer together in a new spirit of common commitment to Euro-Atlantic security and has enabled Partners to participate rapidly and successfully in our broad coalition for peace in Bosnia and Herzegovina. We have therefore decided to substantively enhance the Partnership for Peace and to develop ever-closer and deeper cooperative ties with all interested Partner countries. We have endorsed today a number of additional measures to strengthen political consultation with the Alliance, increase the Partners' involvement in PfP decision-making and planning, and make PfP more operational. This will allow Partner countries to draw closer to the Alliance.

3. We are particularly pleased that on 27th May in Paris our Heads of State and Government and Secretary General Solana signed with President Yeltsin the Founding Act on Mutual Relations, Cooperation and Security between NATO and the Russian Federation. This marks the beginning of a new strong, stable and enduring partnership which will be of vital importance for European security. We are committed to make the Permanent Joint Council a forum for consultation and cooperation for the benefit of stability in the whole of Europe. The activities of the Council will be built upon the principles of reciprocity, transparency and full respect for the interests of other states. We commend the Secretary General and his staff for having achieved this historic agreement for the Alliance.

4. We are satisfied that the preparations for decisions of the Madrid Summit on inviting new members into our Alliance are well on track. We noted a report by the Secretary General reflecting the results of the latest round of the intensified dialogue with interested Partner countries and of the analysis of relevant factors associated with the admission of new members; the necessary adaptation of Alliance structures to integrate new members into the Alliance; and a plan and timetable for the accession talks. These preparations will allow in the weeks to come the formulation of the comprehensive recommendations which we requested at our last meeting. The admission of new members, which will enhance our common security, will involve the Alliance providing the resources which enlargement will necessarily require. We also recommend to our Heads of State and Government to make explicit our commitment that the Alliance remains open to the accession of any other European state able and willing to further the principles of the Washington Treaty and to contribute to our common security. We therefore recommend to our Heads of State and Government that the Madrid Summit should give substance to this commitment.

5. We welcome today's initialling of the Charter on a Distinctive Partnership between NATO and Ukraine and look forward to its signature at the Summit in Madrid. The maintenance of Ukraine's independence, territorial integrity and sovereignty is a crucial factor for stability and security in Europe. We continue to support Ukraine as it develops as a democratic nation and a market economy. We also welcome the opening of the NATO Information Office in Kyiv earlier this month as an important step in further enhancing our relations with Ukraine.

6. We attach great importance to security and stability in the Mediterranean region. We are pleased with the development of the dialogue between NATO and a number of countries of the region. We want to further enhance this dialogue and improve its overall political visibility as an effort

of confidence-building and cooperation that contributes to stability. To this end, we have today agreed a number of measures on the implementation and scope for further development of this dialogue. We have decided to recommend to our Heads of State and Government to formally establish under the authority of the Council a new committee having the overall responsibility for the Mediterranean dialogue.

7.   We welcome the progress made on the Alliance's internal adaptation, guided by the fundamental objectives of ensuring its military effectiveness, preserving the transatlantic link and building the European Security and Defence Identity (ESDI) within the Alliance. We note the progress made on the Long-Term Study on the development of the Alliance's future command structure, underscore the importance of solutions of outstanding issues, and stress the desirability of further developments so that appropriate recommendations for decisions can be submitted to the Madrid Summit in the interest of a timely and successful completion of a new command structure. We note with satisfaction the progress made in implementing the Combined Joint Task Forces (CJTF) concept.

We welcome the substantial progress achieved in the development of the ESDI within the Alliance. We have approved a consolidated interim report, and we direct that further work be pursued vigorously with a view to submitting to our Heads of State and Government in Madrid recommendations for decisions necessary for the successful completion of the internal adaptation of the Alliance.

8.   We welcome agreement reached recently in the WEU on the participation of all European Allies, if they were so to choose, in WEU operations using NATO assets and capabilities, as well as in planning and preparing of such operations; and on involvement, to the fullest extent possible and in accordance with their status, of Observers in the follow-up, within the WEU, of our meetings of Berlin and Brussels. We note that the basis has therefore been established for the implementation of Ministerial decisions, for the strengthening of NATO-WEU working relations and, in this framework, for the development of the ESDI with the full participation of all European Allies. This will, together with decisions taken at the meeting of the WEU Council of Ministers in Paris on 13th May 1997, contribute to setting the groundwork for possible WEU-led operations with the support of Alliance assets and capabilities.

9.   The Alliance's Strategic Concept, adopted by our Heads of State and Government at their meeting in Rome in 1991, sets out the principal aims and objectives of the Alliance. Recognising the changes in the strategic environment since 1991, the Alliance has already decided to examine the

Strategic Concept to ensure that it is fully consistent with Europe's new security situation and challenges. We recommend to our Heads of State and Government at their Madrid Summit to decide the way ahead.

10. We commend the officers and soldiers participating in the Stabilisation Force (SFOR) in Bosnia and Herzegovina for their continued successful contribution to peace in that country.

We recognise that important and demonstrable progress has been made in the overall effort to implement the Peace Agreement since we last met. Municipal elections are scheduled, the sensitive Brcko decision is being implemented, and there have been positive developments in the initiation of joint institutions, the return of refugees and displaced persons, and in economic reconstruction. We are greatly encouraged by the effective cooperation between SFOR and the High Representative and the international organisations and agencies.

Nevertheless, significant challenges remain, and the failure of all the parties to the Peace Agreement to comply fully with their commitments cannot be tolerated. Reaffirming our commitment to the full implementation of the Peace Agreement, we express our serious concern at the lack of determination by the authorities in Bosnia and Herzegovina to honour their obligations and strongly urge them:

- to establish functioning central institutions;
- to ensure freedom of movement, freedom of communication and freedom of the press;
- to respect human rights, the rule of law and the right of all refugees and displaced persons to return freely;
- to cooperate fully with the international community in preparing, conducting and implementing the municipal elections;
- to cooperate with the International Criminal Tribunal for the former Yugoslavia in The Hague in the apprehension and bringing to justice of war criminals;
- to implement fully the provisions of the arms control agreement;
- to adopt and implement the economic measures needed for the functioning of Bosnia and Herzegovina as a single state; and
- to develop democratic, restructured police forces.

We continue to monitor closely the situation in Bosnia and Herzegovina and look forward to the six-month review of SFOR's work in June. We also look forward to the results of tomorrow's Ministerial meeting of the Peace Implementation Council Steering Board.

11. We welcome the initiatives taken in Albania by the OSCE as the coordinating framework for international assistance, as well as by the EU and the

WEU. We commend the Italian-led Multinational Protection Force with the participation of several Allies and Partners which is contributing to creating a secure environment for these initiatives for the re-establishment of peace and order in that country. The elections to be held on 29th June 1997 are an essential step in the process of national reconciliation, and we call on all parties to engage in a constructive dialogue on future democratic reforms in Albania.

12. We welcome entry into force of the CFE Flank Agreement on 15th May 1997. This step underscores the commitment of all States Parties to retain the regional stability ensured by the provisions of the Flank Agreement for the long term in an adapted treaty. We note the progress that has been made toward a Framework Agreement on CFE adaptation and look forward to completion of that task as soon as possible. To this end, we have proposed in Vienna in February 1997 a revised treaty structure of national and territorial ceilings, together with other measures to strengthen overall and regional stability and security throughout Europe. We underline the commitment of all members of the Alliance to the process of adapting the CFE Treaty to a changing security environment, a process which should enhance the security of all States Parties and ensure that the Treaty continues to serve as a cornerstone of European security in the decades to come.

13. We noted with satisfaction the progress report of the Joint Committee on Proliferation (JCP) regarding the activities of the Senior Political-Military Group on Proliferation and the Senior Defence Group on Proliferation. We note the Policy Guidelines for Military Operations in a NBC Weapons Environment developed by the Senior Defence Group on Proliferation. We direct the JCP to continue its vital work. We reaffirm that these political and defence efforts against proliferation remain an integral part of adaptation to the new security environment and welcome further consultations and cooperation with Partner countries to address the common security risks posed by proliferation.

14. We welcome the agreement reached between Presidents Clinton and Yeltsin at Helsinki to reduce strategic nuclear warheads to a level of 2000-2500 in a START III Treaty. We urge the Russian Federation to ratify the START II Treaty promptly so that the negotiations on START III may begin.

15. We are pleased that the Chemical Weapons Convention has entered into force and strongly advocate its full and effective implementation. We call on all states which have not yet signed and ratified the Convention to do so at the earliest possible date.

16. We express our deep appreciation to the Government of Portugal for hosting this meeting.

Madrid Declaration on Euro-Atlantic Security and Cooperation Issued by the Heads of State and Government

1. We, the Heads of State and Government of the member countries of the North Atlantic Alliance, have come together in Madrid to give shape to the new NATO as we move towards the 21st century. Substantial progress has been achieved in the internal adaptation of the Alliance. As a significant step in the evolutionary process of opening the Alliance, we have invited three countries to begin accession talks. We have substantially strengthened our relationship with Partners through the new Euro-Atlantic Partnership Council and enhancement of the Partnership for Peace. The signature on 27th May of the NATO-Russia Founding Act and the Charter we will sign tomorrow with Ukraine bear witness to our commitment to an undivided Europe. We are also enhancing our Mediterranean dialogue. Our aim is to reinforce peace and stability in the Euro-Atlantic area.

   A new Europe is emerging, a Europe of greater integration and cooperation. An inclusive European security architecture is evolving to which we are contributing, along with other European organisations. Our Alliance will continue to be a driving force in this process.

2. We are moving towards the realisation of our vision of a just and lasting order of peace for Europe as a whole, based on human rights, freedom and democracy. In looking forward to the 50th anniversary of the North Atlantic Treaty, we reaffirm our commitment to a strong, dynamic partnership between the European and North American Allies, which has been, and will continue to be, the bedrock of the Alliance and of a free and prosperous Europe. The vitality of the transatlantic link will benefit from the development of a true, balanced partnership in which Europe is taking on greater responsibility. In this spirit, we are building a European Security and Defence Identity within NATO. The Alliance and the European Union share common strategic interests. We welcome the agreements reached at the European Council in Amsterdam. NATO will remain the essential forum for consultation among its members and the venue for agreement on policies bearing on the security and defence commitments of Allies under the Washington Treaty.

3. While maintaining our core function of collective defence, we have adapted our political and military structures to improve our ability to meet the new challenges of regional crisis and conflict management. NATO's continued contribution to peace in Bosnia and Herzegovina, and the unprecedented scale of cooperation with other countries and international organisations there, reflect the cooperative approach which is key to building our common security. A new NATO is developing: a new NATO for a new and undivided Europe.

4. The security of NATO's members is inseparably linked to that of the whole of Europe. Improving the security and stability environment for nations in the Euro-Atlantic area where peace is fragile and instability currently prevails remains a major Alliance interest. The consolidation of democratic and free societies on the entire continent, in accordance with OSCE principles, is therefore of direct and material concern to the Alliance. NATO's policy is to build effective cooperation through its outreach activities, including the Euro-Atlantic Partnership Council, with free nations which share the values of the Alliance, including members of the European Union as well as candidates for EU membership.

5. At our last meeting in Brussels, we said that we would expect and would welcome the accession of new members, as part of an evolutionary process, taking into account political and security developments in the whole of Europe. Twelve European countries have so far requested to join the Alliance. We welcome the aspirations and efforts of these nations. The time has come to start a new phase of this process. The Study on NATO Enlargement—which stated, inter alia, that NATO's military effectiveness should be sustained as the Alliance enlarges—the results of the intensified dialogue with interested Partners, and the analyses of relevant factors associated with the admission of new members have provided a basis on which to assess the current state of preparations of the twelve countries aspiring to Alliance membership.

6. Today, we invite the Czech Republic, Hungary and Poland to begin accession talks with NATO. Our goal is to sign the Protocol of Accession at the time of the Ministerial meetings in December 1997 and to see the ratification process completed in time for membership to become effective by the 50th anniversary of the Washington Treaty in April 1999. During the period leading to accession, the Alliance will involve invited countries, to the greatest extent possible and where appropriate, in Alliance activities, to ensure that they are best prepared to undertake the responsibilities and obligations of membership in an enlarged Alliance. We direct the Council in Permanent Session to develop appropriate arrangements for this purpose.

7. Admitting new members will entail resource implications for the Alliance. It will involve the Alliance providing the resources which enlargement will

necessarily require. We direct the Council in Permanent Session to bring to an early conclusion the concrete analysis of the resource implications of the forthcoming enlargement, drawing on the continuing work on military implications. We are confident that, in line with the security environment of the Europe of today, Alliance costs associated with the integration of new members will be manageable and that the resources necessary to meet those costs will be provided.

8. We reaffirm that NATO remains open to new members under Article 10 of the North Atlantic Treaty. The Alliance will continue to welcome new members in a position to further the principles of the Treaty and contribute to security in the Euro-Atlantic area. The Alliance expects to extend further invitations in coming years to nations willing and able to assume the responsibilities and obligations of membership, and as NATO determines that the inclusion of these nations would serve the overall political and strategic interests of the Alliance and that the inclusion would enhance overall European security and stability. To give substance to this commitment, NATO will maintain an active relationship with those nations that have expressed an interest in NATO membership as well as those who may wish to seek membership in the future. Those nations that have previously expressed an interest in becoming NATO members but that were not invited to begin accession talks today will remain under consideration for future membership. The considerations set forth in our 1995 Study on NATO Enlargement will continue to apply with regard to future aspirants, regardless of their geographic location. No European democratic country whose admission would fulfil the objectives of the Treaty will be excluded from consideration. Furthermore, in order to enhance overall security and stability in Europe, further steps in the ongoing enlargement process of the Alliance should balance the security concerns of all Allies.

To support this process, we strongly encourage the active participation by aspiring members in the Euro-Atlantic Partnership Council and the Partnership for Peace, which will further deepen their political and military involvement in the work of the Alliance. We also intend to continue the Alliance's intensified dialogues with those nations that aspire to NATO membership or that otherwise wish to pursue a dialogue with NATO on membership questions. To this end, these intensified dialogues will cover the full range of political, military, financial and security issues relating to possible NATO membership, without prejudice to any eventual Alliance decision. They will include meeting within the EAPC as well as periodic meetings with the North Atlantic Council in Permanent Session and the NATO

International Staff and with other NATO bodies as appropriate. In keeping with our pledge to maintain an open door to the admission of additional Alliance members in the future, we also direct that NATO Foreign Ministers keep that process under continual review and report to us.

We will review the process at our next meeting in 1999. With regard to the aspiring members, we recognise with great interest and take account of the positive developments towards democracy and the rule of law in a number of southeastern European countries, especially Romania and Slovenia.

The Alliance recognises the need to build greater stability, security and regional cooperation in the countries of southeast Europe, and in promoting their increasing integration into the Euro-Atlantic community. At the same time, we recognise the progress achieved towards greater stability and cooperation by the states in the Baltic region which are also aspiring members. As we look to the future of the Alliance, progress towards these objectives will be important for our overall goal of a free, prosperous and undivided Europe at peace.

9. The establishment of the Euro-Atlantic Partnership Council in Sintra constitutes a new dimension in the relations with our Partners. We look forward to tomorrow's meeting with Heads of State and Government under the aegis of the EAPC.

The EAPC will be an essential element in our common endeavour to enhance security and stability in the Euro-Atlantic region. Building on the successful experience with the North Atlantic Cooperation Council and with Partnership for Peace, it will provide the overarching framework for all aspects of our wide-ranging cooperation and raise it to a qualitatively new level. It will deepen and give more focus to our multilateral political and security-related discussions, enhance the scope and substance of our practical cooperation, and increase transparency and confidence in security matters among all EAPC member states. The expanded political dimension of consultation and cooperation which the EAPC will offer will allow Partners, if they wish, to develop a direct political relationship individually or in smaller groups with the Alliance. The EAPC will increase the scope for consultation and cooperation on regional matters and activities.

10. The Partnership for Peace has become the focal point of our efforts to build new patterns of practical cooperation in the security realm. Without PfP, we would not have been able to put together and deploy so effectively and efficiently the Implementation and Stabilisation Forces in Bosnia and Herzegovina with the participation of so many of our Partners.

We welcome and endorse the decision taken in Sintra to enhance the Partnership for Peace by strengthening the political consultation element, increasing the role Partners play in PfP decision-making and planning, and by making PfP more operational. Partners will, in future, be able to involve themselves more closely in PfP programme issues as well as PfP operations, Partner staff elements will be established at various levels of the military structure of the Alliance, and the Planning and Review Process will become more like the NATO force planning process. On the basis of the principles of inclusiveness and self-differentiation, Partner countries will thus be able to draw closer to the Alliance. We invite all Partner countries to take full advantage of the new possibilities which the enhanced PfP will offer.

With the expanded range of opportunities comes also the need for adequate political and military representation at NATO Headquarters in Brussels. We have therefore created the possibility for Partners to establish diplomatic missions to NATO under the Brussels Agreement which entered into force on 28th March 1997. We invite and encourage Partner countries to take advantage of this opportunity.

11. The Founding Act on Mutual Relations, Cooperation and Security between NATO and the Russian Federation, signed on 27th May 1997 in Paris, is a historic achievement. It opens a new era in European security relations, an era of cooperation between NATO and Russia. The Founding Act reflects our shared commitment to build together a lasting and inclusive peace in the Euro-Atlantic area on the principles of democracy and cooperative security. Its provisions contribute to NATO's underlying objective of enhancing the security of all European states, which is reinforced also through our actions here in Madrid. It provides NATO and Russia a framework through which we intend to create a strong, stable and enduring partnership. We are committed to working with Russia to make full use of the provisions of the Founding Act.

Through the new forum created under the Founding Act, the NATO-Russia Permanent Joint Council, NATO and Russia will consult, cooperate and, where appropriate, act together to address challenges to security in Europe. The activities of the Council will build upon the principles of reciprocity and transparency. The cooperation between Russian and NATO troops in Bosnia and Herzegovina and between the staffs at SHAPE demonstrate what is possible when we work together. We will build on this experience, including through PfP, to develop genuine cooperation between NATO and Russia. We look forward to consulting regularly with Russia on a broad range of topics, and to forging closer cooperation, including military-to-military, through the Permanent Joint Council, which will begin work soon.

12. We attach great importance to tomorrow's signing of the Charter on a Distinctive Partnership between NATO and Ukraine. The NATO-Ukraine Charter will move NATO-Ukraine cooperation onto a more substantive

level, offer new potential for strengthening our relationship, and enhance security in the region more widely. We are convinced that Ukraine's independence, territorial integrity and sovereignty are a key factor for ensuring stability in Europe. We continue to support the reform process in Ukraine as it develops as a democratic nation with a market economy.

We want to build on steps taken to date in developing a strong and enduring relationship between NATO and Ukraine. We welcome the practical cooperation achieved with the Alliance through Ukraine's participation within IFOR and SFOR, as well as the recent opening of the NATO Information Office in Kyiv, as important contributions in this regard. We look forward to the early and active implementation of the Charter.

13. The Mediterranean region merits great attention since security in the whole of Europe is closely linked with security and stability in the Mediterranean. We are pleased with the development of the Mediterranean initiative that was launched following our last meeting in Brussels. The dialogue we have established between NATO and a number of Mediterranean countries is developing progressively and successfully, contributes to confidence-building and cooperation in the region, and complements other international efforts. We endorse the measures agreed by NATO Foreign Ministers in Sintra on the widening of the scope and the enhancement of the dialogue and, on the basis of their recommendation, have decided today to establish under the authority of the North Atlantic Council a new committee, the Mediterranean Cooperation Group, which will have the overall responsibility for the Mediterranean dialogue.

14. We welcome the progress made on the Alliance's internal adaptation. Its fundamental objectives are to maintain the Alliance's military effectiveness and its ability to react to a wide range of contingencies, to preserve the transatlantic link, and develop the European Security and Defence Identity (ESDI) within the Alliance. We recognise the substantive work which has been carried out on the development of a new command structure for the Alliance; the implementation of the Combined Joint Task Forces (CJTF) concept; and the building of ESDI within NATO. We attach great importance to an early and successful completion of this process. Building on the earlier reductions and restructuring of the Alliance's military forces, it will provide the Alliance with the full range of capabilities needed to meet the challenges of the future.

15. We welcome the substantial progress made on the development of a new command structure which will enable the Alliance to carry out the whole range of its missions more effectively and flexibly, support our enhanced relationship with Partners and the admission of new members, and provide, as part of the

development of ESDI within NATO, for European command arrangements able to prepare, support, command and conduct WEU-led operations.

We note that essential elements of the new command structure have been identified and will form the basis for further work. We must maintain the momentum of this work. We have, accordingly, directed the Council in Permanent Session, with the advice of the Military Committee, to work on the resolution of outstanding issues with the aim of reaching agreement on NATO's future command structure by the time of the Council Ministerial meetings in December.

16. Against this background, the members of the Alliance's integrated military structure warmly welcome today's announcement by Spain of its readiness to participate fully in the Alliance's new command structure, once agreement has been reached upon it. Spain's full participation will enhance its overall contribution to the security of the Alliance, help develop the European Security and Defence Identity within NATO and strengthen the transatlantic link.

17. We are pleased with the progress made in implementing the CJTF concept, including the initial designation of parent headquarters, and look forward to the forthcoming trials. This concept will enhance our ability to command and control multinational and multiservice forces, generated and deployed at short notice, which are capable of conducting a wide range of military operations. Combined Joint Task Forces will also facilitate the possible participation of non-NATO nations in operations and, by enabling the conduct of WEU-led CJTF operations, will contribute to the development of ESDI within the Alliance.

18. We reaffirm, as stated in our 1994 Brussels Declaration, our full support for the development of the European Security and Defence Identity by making available NATO assets and capabilities for WEU operations. With this in mind, the Alliance is building ESDI, grounded on solid military principles and supported by appropriate military planning and permitting the creation of militarily coherent and effective forces capable of operating under the political control and strategic direction of the WEU. We endorse the decisions taken at last year's Ministerial meeting in Berlin in this regard which serve the interests of the Alliance as well as of the WEU.

We further endorse the considerable progress made in implementing these decisions and in developing ESDI within the Alliance. In this context we endorse the decisions taken with regard to European command arrangements within NATO to prepare, support, command and conduct WEU-led operations using NATO assets and capabilities (including provisional terms of reference for Deputy SACEUR covering his ESDI-related responsibilities both

permanent and during crises and operations), the arrangements for the identification of NATO assets and capabilities that could support WEU-led operations, and arrangements for NATO-WEU consultation in the context of
such operations. We welcome inclusion of the support for the conduct of
WEU-led operations in the context of the ongoing implementation of the
revised Alliance defence planning process for all Alliance missions. We also
welcome the progress made on work regarding the planning and future exercising of WEU-led operations, and in developing the necessary practical
arrangements for release, monitoring and return of NATO assets and the
exchange of information between NATO and WEU within the framework of
the NATO-WEU Security Agreement.

We note with satisfaction that the building of ESDI within the Alliance has
much benefitted from the recent agreement in the WEU on the participation
of all European Allies, if they were so to choose, in WEU-led operations
using NATO assets and capabilities, as well as in planning and preparing for
such operations. We also note the desire on Canada's part to participate in
such operations when its interests make it desirable and under modalities to
be developed. We direct the Council in Permanent Session to complete expeditiously its work on developing ESDI within NATO, in cooperation with
the WEU.

19. The Alliance Strategic Concept, which we adopted at our meeting in Rome
in 1991, sets out the principal aims and objectives of the Alliance.
Recognising that the strategic environment has changed since then, we have
decided to examine the Strategic Concept to ensure that it is fully consistent
with Europe's new security situation and challenges. As recommended by our
Foreign Ministers in Sintra, we have decided to direct the Council in
Permanent Session to develop terms of reference for this examination, and an
update as necessary, for endorsement at the Autumn Ministerial meetings.
This work will confirm our commitment to the core function of Alliance collective defence and the indispensable transatlantic link.

20. We reiterate our commitment to full transparency between NATO and WEU
in crisis management, including as necessary through joint consultations on
how to address contingencies. In this context, we are determined to
strengthen the institutional cooperation between the two organisations. We
welcome the fact that the WEU has recently undertaken to improve its capacity to plan and conduct crisis management and peacekeeping operations (the
Petersberg tasks), including through setting the groundwork for possible
WEU-led operations with the support of NATO assets and capabilities, and
accepted the Alliance's invitation to contribute to NATO's Ministerial
Guidance for defence planning. We will therefore continue to develop the

arrangements and procedures necessary for the planning, preparation, conduct and exercise of WEU-led operations using NATO assets and capabilities.

21. We reaffirm our commitment to further strengthening the OSCE as a regional organisation according to Chapter VIII of the Charter of the United Nations and as a primary instrument for preventing conflict, enhancing cooperative security and advancing democracy and human rights. The OSCE, as the most inclusive European-wide security organisation, plays an essential role in securing peace, stability and security in Europe. The principles and commitments adopted by the OSCE provide a foundation for the development of a comprehensive and cooperative European security architecture. Our goal is to create in Europe, through the widest possible cooperation among OSCE states, a common space of security and stability, without dividing lines or spheres of influence limiting the sovereignty of particular states.

    We continue to support the OSCE's work on a Common and Comprehensive Security Model for Europe for the Twenty-First Century, in accordance with the decisions of the 1996 Lisbon Summit, including consideration of developing a Charter on European Security.

22. We welcome the successful holding of elections in Albania as a vital first step in providing the basis for greater stability, democratic government and law and order in the country. We stress, in this context, the importance of a firm commitment by all political forces to continue the process of national reconciliation. We also welcome the crucial role of the Italian-led Multinational Protection Force, with the participation of several Allies and Partners, in helping to create a secure environment for the re-establishment of peace and order. We value the efforts of the OSCE as the coordinating framework for international assistance in Albania, together with the important contributions made by the EU, WEU and the Council of Europe. We are following closely events in Albania and are considering measures through the Partnership for Peace to assist, as soon as the situation permits, in the reconstruction of the armed forces of Albania as an important element of the reform process. Continued international support will be essential in helping to restore stability in Albania.

23. We continue to attach greatest importance to further the means of non-proliferation, arms control and disarmament.

    We welcome the progress made since the Brussels Summit, as an integral part of NATO's adaptation, to intensify and expand Alliance political and defence efforts aimed at preventing proliferation and safeguarding NATO's strategic unity and freedom of action despite the risks posed by nuclear, biological and chemical (NBC) weapons and their means of delivery. We attach the utmost importance to these efforts, welcome the Alliance's substantial achievements, and direct that work continue.

We call on all states which have not yet done so to sign and ratify the Chemical Weapons Convention. Recognising that enhancing confidence in compliance would reinforce the Biological and Toxin Weapons Convention, we reaffirm our determination to complete as soon as possible through negotiation a legally binding and effective verification mechanism. We urge the Russian Federation to ratify the START II Treaty without delay so that negotiation of START III may begin.

We support the vigorous pursuit of an effective, legally binding international agreement to ban world-wide the use, stockpiling, production and transfer of anti-personnel mines. We note the positive developments in the Conference on Disarmament. We further note the progress made by the Ottawa Process with its goal of achieving a ban by the end of the year.

24. We continue to attach utmost importance to the CFE Treaty and its integrity. In this context, we welcome the entry into force of the CFE Flank Agreement on 15th May 1997 and underline its importance for regional stability. We share the commitment of all thirty States Parties to continue full implementation of the CFE Treaty, its associated documents, and the Flank Agreement. We confirm our readiness to work cooperatively with other States Parties to achieve, as expeditiously as possible, an adapted CFE Treaty that takes account of the changed political and military circumstances in Europe, continues to serve as a cornerstone of stability, and provides undiminished security for all. NATO has advanced a comprehensive proposal for adaptation of the CFE Treaty on the basis of a revised Treaty structure of national and territorial ceilings. The Allies have already stated their intention to reduce significantly their future aggregate national ceilings for Treaty-Limited Equipment. We look forward to working with other States Parties on the early completion of a Framework Agreement on CFE adaptation.

25. We reaffirm the importance of arrangements in the Alliance for consultation on threats of a wider nature, including those linked to illegal arms trade and acts of terrorism, which affect Alliance security interests. We continue to condemn all acts of international terrorism. They constitute flagrant violations of human dignity and rights and are a threat to the conduct of normal international relations. In accordance with our national legislation, we stress the need for the most effective cooperation possible to prevent and suppress this scourge.

26. The steps we have taken today, and tomorrow's meeting with our Partners under the aegis of the EAPC, bring us closer to our goal of building cooperative security in Europe. We remain committed to a free and undivided

Euro-Atlantic community in which all can enjoy peace and prosperity. Renewed in structure and approach, strengthened in purpose and resolve, and with a growing membership, NATO will continue to play its part in achieving this goal and in meeting the security challenges in the times ahead.

27. We express our deep appreciation for the gracious hospitality extended to us by the Government of Spain. We are looking forward to meeting again on the occasion of the 50th anniversary of the North Atlantic Treaty in April 1999.

The Washington Declaration Signed and issued by the Heads of State and Government participating in the meeting of the North Atlantic Council in Washington D.C. on 23rd and 24th April 1999

1. We, the Heads of State and Government of the member countries of the North Atlantic Alliance, declare for a new century our mutual commitment to defend our people, our territory and our liberty, founded on democracy, human rights and the rule of law. The world has changed dramatically over the last half century, but our common values and security interests remain the same.

2. At this anniversary summit, we affirm our determination to continue advancing these goals, building on the habits of trust and co-operation we have developed over fifty years. Collective defence remains the core purpose of NATO. We affirm our commitment to promote peace, stability and freedom.

3. We pay tribute to the men and women who have served our Alliance and who have advanced the cause of freedom. To honour them and to build a better future, we will contribute to building a stronger and broader Euro-Atlantic community of democracies—a community where human rights and fundamental freedoms are upheld; where borders are increasingly open to people, ideas and commerce; where war becomes unthinkable.

4. We reaffirm our faith, as stated in the North Atlantic Treaty, in the purposes and principles of the Charter of the United Nations and reiterate our desire to live in peace with all nations, and to settle any international dispute by peaceful means.

5. We must be as effective in the future in dealing with new challenges as we were in the past. We are charting NATO's course as we enter the 21st century: an Alliance committed to collective defence, capable of addressing current and future risks to our security, strengthened by and open to new members, and working together with other institutions, Partners and Mediterranean Dialogue countries in a mutually reinforcing way to enhance Euro-Atlantic security and stability.

6. NATO embodies the vital partnership between Europe and North America. We welcome the further impetus that has been given to the strengthening of European defence capabilities to enable the European Allies to act more effectively together, thus reinforcing the transatlantic partnership.

7. We remain determined to stand firm against those who violate human rights, wage war and conquer territory. We will maintain both the political solidarity and the military forces necessary to protect our nations and to meet the security challenges of the next century. We pledge to improve our defence capabilities to fulfil the full range of the Alliance's 21st century missions. We will continue to build confidence and security through arms control, disarmament and non-proliferation measures. We reiterate our condemnation of terrorism and our determination to protect ourselves against this scourge.

8. Our Alliance remains open to all European democracies, regardless of geography, willing and able to meet the responsibilities of membership, and whose inclusion would enhance overall security and stability in Europe. NATO is an essential pillar of a wider community of shared values and shared responsibility. Working together, Allies and Partners, including Russia and Ukraine, are developing their cooperation and erasing the divisions imposed by the Cold War to help to build a Europe whole and free, where security and prosperity are shared and indivisible.

9. Fifty years after NATO's creation, the destinies of North America and Europe remain inseparable. When we act together, we safeguard our freedom and security and enhance stability more effectively than any of us could alone. Now, and for the century about to begin, we declare as the fundamental objectives of this Alliance enduring peace, security and liberty for all people of Europe and North America.

Membership Action Plan (MAP)

1.   The door to NATO membership under Article 10 of the North Atlantic Treaty remains open. The Membership Action Plan (MAP), building on the Intensified, Individual Dialogue on membership questions, is designed to reinforce that firm commitment to further enlargement by putting into place a programme of activities to assist aspiring countries in their preparations for possible future membership. It must be understood that decisions made by aspirants on the basis of advice received will remain national decisions undertaken and implemented at the sole responsibility of the country concerned.

2.   The programme offers aspirants a list of activities from which they may select those they consider of most value to help them in their preparations. Active participation in PfP and EAPC mechanisms remains essential for aspiring countries who wish to further deepen their political and military involvement in the work of the Alliance.

3.   Any decision to invite an aspirant to begin accession talks with the Alliance will be made on a case-by-case basis by Allies in accordance with paragraph 8 of the Madrid Summit Declaration, and the Washington Summit Declaration. Participation in the Membership Action Plan, which would be on the basis of self-differentiation, does not imply any timeframe for any such decision nor any guarantee of eventual membership. The programme cannot be considered as a list of criteria for membership.

Implementation

1.   The Membership Action Plan, which is a practical manifestation of the Open Door, is divided into five chapters. These chapters are:

I.   Political and Economic issues

II.   Defence/Military issues

III. Resource issues

IV.   Security issues

V.   Legal issues

Within each, the MAP identifies issues that might be discussed (non-exhaustive) and highlights mechanisms through which preparation for possible eventual membership can best be carried forward.

The list of issues identified for discussion does not constitute criteria for membership and is intended to encompass those issues which the aspiring countries themselves have identified as matters which they wish to address.

2. Each aspiring country will be requested to draw up an annual national programme on preparations for possible future membership, setting objectives and targets for its preparations and containing specific information on steps being taken, the responsible authorities and, where appropriate, a schedule of work on specific aspects of those preparations. It would be open to aspirants to update the programme when they chose. The programme would form a basis for the Alliance to keep track of aspirants' progress and to provide feedback.

3. Meetings will take place in a 19+1 format in the Council and other bodies and in NATO IS/NMA Team formats as appropriate.

4. Feedback and advice to aspirants on MAP issues will be provided through mechanisms based on those currently in use for Partners, 19+1 meetings and NATO Team workshops. These workshops will be held, when justified, to discuss particular issues drawn from the MAP.

5. The NATO Team will normally be headed by the appropriate Assistant Secretary General, Assistant Director of the International Military Staff, Head of Office or his representative. The NATO Team will liaise closely with the appropriate NATO bodies regarding advice to aspirants. Relevant procedures will be refined over time as experience is gained. Aspirants should make requests in writing for workshops to ASG/PA. He will be responsible for the implementation of the Membership Action Plan and the scheduling of meetings under the overall direction and coordination of the SPC(R).

6. Each year the Alliance will draw up for individual aspirants a report providing feedback focused on progress made in the areas covered in their annual national programmes. This document would form the basis of discussion at a meeting of the North Atlantic Council with the aspirant country. The report would help identify areas for further action, but it would remain at the aspirant's discretion to commit itself to taking further action.

I. Political and Economic Issues

1. Aspirants would be offered the opportunity to discuss and substantiate their willingness and ability to assume the obligations and commitments under the Washington Treaty and the relevant provisions of the Study on NATO Enlargement. Future members must conform to basic principles embodied in the Washington Treaty such as democracy, individual liberty and other relevant provisions set out in its Preamble.

2. Aspirants would also be expected:
   a. to settle their international disputes by peaceful means;

b. to demonstrate commitment to the rule of law and human rights;

c. to settle ethnic disputes or external territorial disputes including irredentist claims or internal jurisdictional disputes by peaceful means in accordance with OSCE principles and to pursue good neighbourly relations;

d. to establish appropriate democratic and civilian control of their armed forces;

e. to refrain from the threat or use of force in any manner inconsistent with the purposes of the UN;

f. to contribute to the development of peaceful and friendly international relations by strengthening their free institutions and by promoting stability and well-being;

g. to continue fully to support and be engaged in the Euro-Atlantic Partnership Council and the Partnership for Peace;

h. to show a commitment to promoting stability and well-being by economic liberty, social justice and environmental responsibility.

3. Moreover, aspirants would be expected upon accession:

a. to unite their efforts for collective defence and for the preservation of peace and security;

b. to maintain the effectiveness of the Alliance through the sharing of responsibilities, costs and benefits;

c. to commit themselves to good faith efforts to build consensus on all issues;

d. to undertake to participate fully in the Alliance consultation and decision-making process on political and security issues of concern to the Alliance;

e. to commit themselves to the continued openness of the Alliance in accordance with the Washington Treaty and the Madrid and Washington Summit Declarations.

Implementation

4. Aspirants will be expected to describe how their policies and practice are evolving to reflect the considerations set out above (in paragraphs 1-2 above), and to provide their views on, and substantiate their willingness and ability to comply with other parts of the NATO "acquis", including the NATO Strategic Concept, the development of the European Security and Defence Identity within the Alliance, the NATO-Russia Founding Act and the NATO-Ukraine Charter.

5. Aspirants would be expected to provide information on an annual basis on the state of their economy, including main macro-economic and budgetary data as well as pertinent economic policy developments.

6. Aspirants would be asked to provide a written contribution to the NATO Team, which would then be passed directly on to the Allies for their comments. After appropriate consultation in the Alliance, the NATO Team would then convene a meeting to discuss the contribution provided and relevant political issues. Such meetings would be held yearly; additional meetings could be convened upon mutual agreement.

7. An annual Senior Political Committee (Reinforced) meeting will be held to provide direct feedback from Allies to individual aspirants.

II. Defence/Military Issues

1. The ability of aspiring countries to contribute militarily to collective defence and to the Alliance's new missions and their willingness to commit to gradual improvements in their military capabilities will be factors to be considered in determining their suitability for NATO membership. Full participation in operational PfP is an essential component, as it will further deepen aspirants' political and military ties with the Alliance, helping them prepare for participation in the full range of new missions. New members of the Alliance must be prepared to share the roles, risks, responsibilities, benefits and burdens of common security and collective defence. They should be expected to subscribe to Alliance strategy as set out in the Strategic Concept and as laid out in other Ministerial statements.

2. Aspirants would be expected upon accession:
   a. to accept the approach to security outlined in the Strategic Concept;
   b. to provide forces and capabilities for collective defence and other Alliance missions;
   c. to participate, as appropriate, in the military structure;
   d. to participate, as appropriate, in the Alliance's collective defence planning;
   e. to participate, as appropriate, in NATO agencies;
   f. to continue fully to support PfP and the development of cooperative relations with non-NATO Partners;
   g. to pursue standardization and/or interoperability.

Implementation

3. The following measures are designed to help aspirants develop the capabilities of their armed forces, including by enhancing interoperability, to be able to contribute to the effectiveness of the Alliance and thus demonstrate their suitability for future membership. The measures build where possible on extant initiatives.
   a. Aspirants will be able in accordance with existing PfP procedures to request tailored Individual Partnership Programmes to better focus

their participation in PfP directly on the essential membership related issues. Within each IPP, certain generic areas would be marked as being essential for aspirants, and aspirants would be invited to give due priority to those areas of cooperation.

b. Annual Clearinghouse meetings for aspirants in a 19+1 format would be developed to help coordinate bilateral and multilateral assistance and maximise their mutual effectiveness to better assist them in their preparations for membership.

c. Within the general framework of the expanded and adapted PARP and in accordance with PARP procedures, planning targets specifically covering areas most directly relevant for nations preparing their force structures and capabilities for possible future Alliance membership will be elaborated with aspirants. Aspirants will undergo a review process on their progress in meeting these planning targets.

d. These planning targets will be established on the basis of consultations between each aspiring country and NATO and may be applied to any component of their force structures, rather than solely to their PfP-declared forces.

e. PARP Ministerial Guidance will include approaches and specific measures which aspirants might adopt, in the context of the MAP, to prepare their forces for possible future NATO membership.

f. The PARP Survey will be used for aspirants to seek more information and data in a number of areas, for example, general defence policy, resources, and present and planned outlays for defence.

g. As a sign of transparency, and in accordance with PARP procedures: aspirants will be encouraged to circulate individual PARP documents to other aspirants in addition to circulating them to NATO Allies; and aspirants will be encouraged to invite, in particular, other aspiring countries to participate in the review process on planning targets.

h. Aspirants will be invited to observe and participate in selected, clearly defined phases of NATO-only exercises when Council decides to open these in accordance with current procedures. Priority consideration will be given to ensuring exercise effectiveness.

i. Any future NATO facilities established for the assessment of Partner forces for NATO-led peace support operations and of Partner performance in NATO/PfP exercises and operations will be used to assess the degree of interoperability and the range of capabilities of aspirants' forces. If these assessment facilities are extended to encompass forces beyond those for peace support operations, they will be used to assist aspirants.

j. Appropriate use may be made of simulation technology for training forces and procedures.

III. Resource Issues

1. New Alliance members would be expected to commit sufficient budget resources to allow themselves to meet the commitments entailed by possible membership. National programmes of aspirants must put in place the necessary structures to plan and implement defence budgets that meet established defence priorities and make provision for training schemes to familiarise staff with NATO practices and procedures in order to prepare for possible future participation in Alliance structures.

2. Aspirants would be expected upon accession:
    a. to allocate sufficient budget resources for the implementation of Alliance commitments;
    b. to have the national structures in place to deal with those budget resources;
    c. to participate in the Alliance's common-funded activities at agreed cost shares;
    d. to participate in Alliance structures (permanent representation at the NATO HQ; military representation in the NATO command structure; participation, as appropriate, in NATO Agencies).

Implementation

3. Through existing mechanisms, including those within PfP, possible internships and training sessions, and NATO Team workshops, aspirants upon request will be:
    a. provided advice on their development of national structures, procedures and mechanisms to deal with the above issues and to ensure the most efficient use of their defence spending;
    b. assisted in training the staff needed to man those structures and work in and with NATO.

IV. Security Issues

1. Aspirants would be expected upon accession to have in place sufficient safeguards and procedures to ensure the security of the most sensitive information as laid down in NATO security policy.

Implementation

2. Appropriate courses may be made available, on request, to aspiring countries on Personnel, Physical, Document, Industrial Security and INFOSEC. Individual programmes for aspirants may be developed as warranted. The NATO Security and Special Committees may wish to meet with aspirants, whenever they judge it necessary or useful.

V. Legal issues

1. In order to be able to undertake the commitments of membership, aspirants should examine and become acquainted with the appropriate legal arrangements and agreements which govern cooperation within NATO. This should enable aspirants to scrutinize domestic law for compatibility with those NATO rules and regulations. In addition, aspirants should be properly informed about the formal legal process leading to membership.

   a. New members, upon completion of the relevant procedures, will accede to:

      The North Atlantic Treaty (Washington, 4th April 1949)

   b. Upon invitation, new members should accede to:

      i. The Agreement between the Parties to the North Atlantic Treaty regarding the status of their forces (London SOFA) (London, 19th June 1951)

      ii. The Protocol on the status of International Military Headquarters set up pursuant to the North Atlantic Treaty (Paris Protocol) (Paris, 28th August 1952)

   c. It is expected that new members accede to the following status agreements:

      i. The Agreement on the status of the North Atlantic Treaty Organization, National Representatives and International Staff (Ottawa Agreement) (Ottawa, 20th September 1951)

      ii. The Agreement on the status of Missions and Representatives of third States to the North Atlantic Treaty Organization (Brussels Agreement) (Brussels, 14th September 1994)

   d. It is expected that new members accede to the following technical agreements:

      i. The Agreement between the Parties to the North Atlantic Treaty for the Security of Information (Brussels, 6th March 1997)

      ii. The Agreement for the mutual safeguarding of secrecy of inventions relation to defence and for which applications for patents have been made (Paris, 21st September 1960)

      iii. The NATO Agreement on the communication of technical information for defence purposes (Brussels, 19th October 1970)

   e. For possible eventual access to ATOMAL information, new members would be expected to accede to:

      i. the "Agreement for Cooperation Regarding Atomic Information" (C-M(64)39—Basic Agreement);

      ii. the "Administrative Arrangements to Implement the Agreement" (C-M(68)41, 5th Revise);

    f.   Domestic legislation of aspirants should, as much as possible, be compatible with the other arrangements and implementation practices which govern NATO-wide cooperation.

Implementation

    2.   NATO Team workshops will provide for briefings on legal issues and discussions on the steps that would have to be taken. Aspirants could provide information on existing legal arrangements and the steps that would have to be taken to accede to the agreements, including whether or not there are any constitutional/legal barriers to doing so.

    3.   Aspirants might also provide information on whether and how domestic legislation might impede immediate and full integration into Alliance activities. Exchange of information and experience on this issue could take place with all aspirants as appropriate.

Prague Summit Declaration Issued by the Heads of State and Government participating in the meeting of the North Atlantic Council in Prague on 21 November 2002

1. We, the Heads of State and Government of the member countries of the North Atlantic Alliance, met today to enlarge our Alliance and further strengthen NATO to meet the grave new threats and profound security challenges of the 21st century. Bound by our common vision embodied in the Washington Treaty, we commit ourselves to transforming NATO with new members, new capabilities and new relationships with our partners. We are steadfast in our commitment to the transatlantic link; to NATO's fundamental security tasks including collective defence; to our shared democratic values; and to the United Nations Charter.

2. Today, we have decided to invite Bulgaria, Estonia, Latvia, Lithuania, Romania, Slovakia and Slovenia to begin accession talks to join our Alliance. We congratulate them on this historic occasion, which so fittingly takes place in Prague. The accession of these new members will strengthen security for all in the Euro-Atlantic area, and help achieve our common goal of a Europe whole and free, united in peace and by common values. NATO's door will remain open to European democracies willing and able to assume the responsibilities and obligations of membership, in accordance with Article 10 of the Washington Treaty.

3. Recalling the tragic events of 11 September 2001 and our subsequent decision to invoke Article 5 of the Washington Treaty, we have approved a comprehensive package of measures, based on NATO's Strategic Concept, to strengthen our ability to meet the challenges to the security of our forces, populations and territory, from wherever they may come. Today's decisions will provide for balanced and effective capabilities within the Alliance so that NATO can better carry out the full range of its missions and respond collectively to those challenges, including the threat posed by terrorism and by the proliferation of weapons of mass destruction and their means of delivery.

4. We underscore that our efforts to transform and adapt NATO should not be perceived as a threat by any country or organisation, but rather as a demonstration of our determination to protect our populations, territory and forces from any armed attack, including terrorist attack, directed from abroad. We are determined to deter, disrupt, defend and protect against any attacks on us, in accordance with the Washington Treaty and the Charter of the United Nations. In order to carry out the full range of its missions, NATO must be able to field forces that can move quickly to wherever they are needed, upon decision by the North Atlantic Council, to sustain operations over distance and time, including in an environment where they might be faced with nuclear, biological and chemical threats, and to achieve their objectives. Effective military forces, an essential part of our overall political strategy, are vital to safeguard the freedom and security of our populations and to contribute to peace and security in the Euro-Atlantic region. We have therefore decided to:

a. Create a NATO Response Force (NRF) consisting of a technologically advanced, flexible, deployable, interoperable and sustainable force including land, sea, and air elements ready to move quickly to wherever needed, as decided by the Council. The NRF will also be a catalyst for focusing and promoting improvements in the Alliance's military capabilities. We gave directions for the development of a comprehensive concept for such a force, which will have its initial operational capability as soon as possible, but not later than October 2004 and its full operational capability not later than October 2006, and for a report to Defence Ministers in Spring 2003. The NRF and the related work of the EU Headline Goal should be mutually reinforcing while respecting the autonomy of both organisations.

b. Streamline NATO's military command arrangements. We have approved the Defence Ministers' report providing the outline of a leaner, more efficient, effective and deployable command structure, with a view to meeting the operational requirements for the full range of Alliance missions. It is based on the agreed Minimum Military Requirements document for the Alliance's command arrangements. The structure will enhance the transatlantic link, result in a significant reduction in headquarters and Combined Air Operations Centres, and promote the transformation of our military capabilities. There will be two strategic commands, one operational, and one functional. The strategic command for Operations, headquartered in Europe (Belgium), will be supported by two Joint Force Commands able to generate a land-based Combined Joint Task Force (CJTF) headquarters and a robust but more limited standing joint headquarters from which a sea-based CJTF headquarters capability can be drawn. There will also be land, sea and air components. The strategic command for Transformation, headquartered in the United States, and with a presence in Europe, will be responsible for the continuing transformation of military capabilities and for the promotion of interoperability of Alliance forces, in cooperation with the Allied Command Operations as appropriate. We have instructed the Council and Defence Planning Committee, taking into account the work of the NATO Military Authorities and objective military criteria, to finalise the details of the structure, including geographic locations of command structure headquarters and other elements, so that final decisions are taken by Defence Ministers in June 2003.

c.　Approve the Prague Capabilities Commitment (PCC) as part of the continuing Alliance effort to improve and develop new military capabilities for modern warfare in a high threat environment. Individual Allies have made firm and specific political commitments to improve their capabilities in the areas of chemical, biological, radiological, and nuclear defence; intelligence, surveillance, and target acquisition; air-to-ground surveillance; command, control and communications; combat effectiveness, including precision guided munitions and suppression of enemy air defences; strategic air and sea lift; air-to-air refuelling; and deployable combat support and combat service support units. Our efforts to improve capabilities through the PCC and those of the European Union to enhance European capabilities through the European Capabilities Action Plan should be mutually reinforcing, while respecting the autonomy of both organisations, and in a spirit of openness.

We will implement all aspects of our Prague Capabilities Commitment as quickly as possible. We will take the necessary steps to improve capabilities in the identified areas of continuing capability shortfalls. Such steps could include multinational efforts, role specialisation and reprioritisation, noting that in many cases additional financial resources will be required, subject as appropriate to parliamentary approval. We are committed to pursuing vigorously capability improvements. We have directed the Council in Permanent Session to report on implementation to Defence Ministers.

d.　Endorse the agreed military concept for defence against terrorism. The concept is part of a package of measures to strengthen NATO's capabilities in this area, which also includes improved intelligence sharing and crisis response arrangements.

Terrorism, which we categorically reject and condemn in all its forms and manifestations, poses a grave and growing threat to Alliance populations, forces and territory, as well as to international security. We are determined to combat this scourge for as long as necessary. To combat terrorism effectively, our response must be multi-faceted and comprehensive.

We are committed, in cooperation with our partners, to fully implement the Civil Emergency Planning (CEP) Action Plan for the improvement of civil preparedness against possible attacks against the civilian population with chemical, biological or radiological (CBR) agents. We will enhance our ability to provide support, when requested, to help national authorities to deal with the consequences of terrorist attacks, including attacks with CBRN against critical infrastructure, as foreseen in the CEP Action Plan.

e. Endorse the implementation of five nuclear, biological and chemical weapons defence initiatives, which will enhance the Alliance's defence capabilities against weapons of mass destruction: a Prototype Deployable NBC Analytical Laboratory; a Prototype NBC Event Response team; a virtual Centre of Excellence for NBC Weapons Defence; a NATO Biological and Chemical Defence Stockpile; and a Disease Surveillance system. We reaffirm our commitment to augment and improve expeditiously our NBC defence capabilities.

f. Strengthen our capabilities to defend against cyber attacks.

g. Examine options for addressing the increasing missile threat to Alliance territory, forces and population centres in an effective and efficient way through an appropriate mix of political and defence efforts, along with deterrence. Today we initiated a new NATO Missile Defence feasibility study to examine options for protecting Alliance territory, forces and population centres against the full range of missile threats, which we will continue to assess. Our efforts in this regard will be consistent with the indivisibility of Allied security. We support the enhancement of the role of the WMD Centre within the International Staff to assist the work of the Alliance in tackling this threat.

We reaffirm that disarmament, arms control and non-proliferation make an essential contribution to preventing the spread and use of WMD and their means of delivery. We stress the importance of abiding by and strengthening existing multilateral non-proliferation and export control regimes and international arms control and disarmament accords.

5. Admitting Bulgaria, Estonia, Latvia, Lithuania, Romania, Slovakia and Slovenia as new members will enhance NATO's ability to face the challenges of today and tomorrow. They have demonstrated their commitment to the

basic principles and values set out in the Washington Treaty, the ability to contribute to the Alliance's full range of missions including collective defence, and a firm commitment to contribute to stability and security, especially in regions of crisis and conflict. We will begin accession talks immediately with the aim of signing Accession Protocols by the end of March 2003 and completing the ratification process in time for these countries to join the Alliance at the latest at our Summit in May 2004. During the period leading up to accession, the Alliance will involve the invited countries in Alliance activities to the greatest extent possible. We pledge our continued support and assistance, including through the Membership Action Plan (MAP). We look forward to receiving the invitees' timetables for reforms, upon which further progress will be expected before and after accession in order to enhance their contribution to the Alliance.

6. We commend Albania for its significant reform progress, its constructive role in promoting regional stability, and strong support for the Alliance. We commend the former Yugoslav Republic of Macedonia[1] for the significant progress it has achieved in its reform process and for its strong support for Alliance operations, as well as for the important steps it has made in overcoming its internal challenges and advancing democracy, stability and ethnic reconciliation. We will continue to help both countries, including through the MAP, to achieve stability, security and prosperity, so that they can meet the obligations of membership. In this context, we have also agreed to improve our capacity to contribute to Albania's continued reform, and to further assist defence and security sector reform in the former Yugoslav Republic of Macedonia through the NATO presence. We encourage both countries to redouble their reform efforts. They remain under consideration for future membership.

7. Croatia, which has made encouraging progress on reform, will also be under consideration for future membership. Progress in this regard will depend upon Croatia's further reform efforts and compliance with all of its international obligations, including to the International Criminal Tribunal for the former Yugoslavia (ICTY).

The Membership Action Plan will remain the vehicle to keep aspirants' progress under review. Today's invitees will not be the last.

The Euro-Atlantic Partnership Council (EAPC) and the Partnership for Peace (PfP) have greatly enhanced security and stability throughout the Euro-Atlantic area. We have today decided to upgrade our cooperation with the EAPC/PfP countries. Our political dialogue will be strengthened, and Allies, in consultation with Partners, will, to the maximum extent possible, increase involvement of Partners, as appropriate, in the planning, conduct, and oversight of those activities and projects in which they participate and to which they contribute. We have introduced new practical mechanisms, such as Individual Partnership Action Plans, which will ensure a comprehensive, tailored and differentiated approach to the Partnership, and which allow for support to the reform efforts of Partners. We encourage Partners, including the countries of the strategically important regions of the Caucasus and Central Asia, to take advantage of these mechanisms. We welcome the resolve of Partners to undertake all efforts to combat terrorism, including through the Partnership Action Plan against Terrorism. We will also continue to further enhance interoperability and defence-related activities, which constitute the core of our partnership. Participation in the PfP and the EAPC could be broadened in the future to include the Federal Republic of Yugoslavia and Bosnia and Herzegovina once necessary progress is achieved, including full cooperation with the ICTY.

8. We welcome the significant achievements of the NATO-Russia Council since the historic NATO-Russia Summit meeting in Rome. We have deepened our relationship to the benefit of all the peoples in the Euro-Atlantic area. NATO member states and Russia are working together in the NATO-Russia Council as equal partners, making progress in areas such as peacekeeping, defence reform, WMD proliferation, search and rescue, civil emergency planning, theatre missile defence and the struggle against terrorism, towards our shared goal of a stable, peaceful and undivided Europe. In accordance with the Founding Act and the Rome Declaration, we are determined to intensify and broaden our cooperation with Russia.

9. We remain committed to strong NATO-Ukraine relations under the Charter on a Distinctive Partnership. We note Ukraine's determination to pursue full Euro-Atlantic integration, and encourage Ukraine to implement all the reforms necessary, including as regards enforcement of export controls, to achieve this objective. The new Action Plan that we are adopting with Ukraine is an important step forward; it identifies political, economic, military and other reform areas where Ukraine is committed to make further progress and where NATO will continue to assist. Continued progress in deepening and enhancing our relationship requires an unequivocal Ukrainian commitment to the values of the Euro-Atlantic community.

10. We reaffirm that security in Europe is closely linked to security and stability in the Mediterranean. We therefore decide to upgrade substantially the political and practical dimensions of our Mediterranean Dialogue as an integral part of the Alliance's cooperative approach to security. In this respect, we encourage intensified practical cooperation and effective interaction on security matters of common concern, including terrorism-related issues, as

appropriate, where NATO can provide added value. We reiterate that the Mediterranean Dialogue and other international efforts, including the EU Barcelona process, are complementary and mutually reinforcing.

11. NATO and the European Union share common strategic interests. We remain strongly committed to the decisions made at the Washington Summit and subsequent Ministerial meetings, in order to enhance NATO-EU cooperation. The success of our cooperation has been evident in our concerted efforts in the Balkans to restore peace and create the conditions for prosperous and democratic societies. Events on and since 11 September 2001 have underlined further the importance of greater transparency and cooperation between our two organisations on questions of common interest relating to security, defence, and crisis management, so that crises can be met with the most appropriate military response and effective crisis management ensured. We remain committed to making the progress needed on all the various aspects of our relationship, noting the need to find solutions satisfactory to all Allies on the issue of participation by non-EU European Allies, in order to achieve a genuine strategic partnership.

12. To further promote peace and stability in the Euro-Atlantic Area, NATO will continue to develop its fruitful and close cooperation with the OSCE, namely in the complementary areas of conflict prevention, crisis management and post-conflict rehabilitation.

13. The Alliance has played a vital role in restoring a secure environment in South-East Europe. We reaffirm our support for the territorial integrity and sovereignty of all the countries in this strategically important region. We will continue to work with our partners in SFOR and KFOR, the United Nations, the European Union, the OSCE and other international organisations, to help build a peaceful, stable and democratic South-East Europe, where all countries assume ownership of the process of reform, and are integrated in Euro-Atlantic structures. We remain determined to see that goal become reality. We expect the countries of the region: to continue to build enduring multi-ethnic democracies, root out organised crime and corruption and firmly establish the rule of law; to cooperate regionally; and to comply fully with international obligations, including by bringing to justice in The Hague all ICTY indictees. The reform progress that these countries make will determine the pace of their integration into Euro-Atlantic structures. We confirm our continued presence in the region and we stand ready to assist these countries in the region, through individual programmes of assistance, to continue their progress. In the light of continuing progress and analysis of the prevailing security and political environment, we will explore options for a further rationalisation and force restructuring, taking into account a

regional approach. We welcome the successful conclusion of Operation Amber Fox in the former Yugoslav Republic of Macedonia. We have agreed to maintain a NATO presence from 15 December for a limited period to contribute to continuing stability, which we will review in the light of the evolving situation. We note the EU's expressed readiness to take over the military operation in the former Yugoslav Republic of Macedonia under appropriate conditions.

14. NATO member countries have responded to the call of the UN Security Council to assist the Afghan government in restoring security in Kabul and its surroundings. Their forces constitute the backbone of the International Security Assistance Force (ISAF) in Afghanistan. We commend the United Kingdom and Turkey for their successive contributions as ISAF lead nations, and welcome the willingness of Germany and the Netherlands jointly to succeed them. NATO has agreed to provide support in selected areas for the next ISAF lead nations, showing our continued commitment. However, the responsibility for providing security and law and order throughout Afghanistan resides with the Afghans themselves.

15. We remain committed to the CFE Treaty and reaffirm our attachment to the early entry into force of the Adapted Treaty. The CFE regime provides a fundamental contribution to a more secure and integrated Europe. We welcome the approach of those non-CFE countries, which have stated their intention to request accession to the Adapted CFE Treaty upon its entry into force. Their accession would provide an important additional contribution to European stability and security. We welcome the significant results of Russia's effort to reduce forces in the Treaty's Article V area to agreed levels. We urge swift fulfilment of the outstanding Istanbul commitments on Georgia and Moldova, which will create the conditions for Allies and other States Parties to move forward on ratification of the Adapted CFE Treaty.

16. As NATO transforms, we have endorsed a package of measures to improve the efficiency and effectiveness of the headquarters organisation. The NATO+Initiative on human resources issues complements this effort. We are committed to continuing to provide, individually and collectively, the resources that are necessary to allow our Alliance to perform the tasks that we demand of it.

17. We welcome the role of the NATO Parliamentary Assembly in complementing NATO's efforts to project stability throughout Europe. We also appreciate the contribution made by the Atlantic Treaty Association in promoting better understanding of the Alliance and its objectives among our publics.

18. We express our deep appreciation for the gracious hospitality extended to us by the Government of the Czech Republic.

19. Our Summit demonstrates that European and North American Allies, already united by history and common values, will remain a community determined and able to defend our territory, populations and forces against all threats and challenges. For over fifty years, NATO has defended peace, democracy and security in the Euro-Atlantic area. The commitments we have undertaken here in Prague will ensure that the Alliance continues to play that vital role into the future.

1. Turkey recognises the Republic of Macedonia with its constitutional name.

0-595-27969-4